Her World
of
Darkness and *Pain*

Bullying and Self-Esteem

Laketta Lowery

abbott press®

A DIVISION OF WRITER'S DIGEST

Her World of Darkness and Pain
Bullying and Self-Esteem

Abbott Press books may be ordered through booksellers or by contacting:

Abbott Press
1663 Liberty Drive
Bloomington, IN 47403
www.abbottpress.com
Phone: 1-866-697-5310

Because of the dynamic nature of the Internet, any web addresses or links contained in this book may have changed since publication and may no longer be valid. The views expressed in this work are solely those of the author and do not necessarily reflect the views of the publisher, and the publisher hereby disclaims any responsibility for them.

Any people depicted in stock imagery provided by Thinkstock are models, and such images are being used for illustrative purposes only.

Certain stock imagery © Thinkstock.

ISBN: 978-1-4582-0284-0 (sc)
ISBN: 978-1-4582-0283-3 (e)

Library of Congress Control Number: 2012904455

Printed in the United States of America

Abbott Press rev. date:3/27/2012

INTRODUCTION

Bullying is a worldwide epidemic. It is becoming a serious issue everyday especially in schools. Children face bullies on a daily basis. Bullying can affect a person in many different ways. The long-term effects can be detrimental to a person's life. There are different types of bullying: 1) physical bullying, 2) emotional bullying 3) verbal bullying and 4) cyber bullying. Bullying can lead to suicide, depression, and low self-esteem. What people fail to realize is the person doing the bullying needs more help than the victim does. It is important to create strategies and interventions for the bully as well as the victim. Will bullying ever stop? Of course not, but that does not mean WE should not put forth the effort to come up with a solution to the problem. Do parents, teachers, counselors, and administrators do all they can to prevent bullying? Do schools educate children on bullying? Honestly, some do and some do not. Everyone always talk the talk, but no one is willing to walk the walk. Society talks about world peace, improving schools, and educating children the best way possible, but do WE actually put in work. Bullying is no different than a drug addiction, alcoholism, or gambling addiction. Today's youth does not know how to deal with problems they face. They want to take the easy way out. All they know how to do is send text messages and talk on the internet. Communication is the key to everything, especially face to face. It is amazing how today's society can text or email anything to someone, but when face to face, there is complete silence! Today's technology keeps children from learning how to communicate and WE wonder why more and more children are committing suicide, shooting up schools, and bullying! I would like you to sit back, relax, and embrace yourself as I take you on the journey of my bullying experiences and the long-term effects it has had on my life.

DEDICATION

This book is dedicated to anyone who is being bullied, has been bullied, and the parents who have children being bullied. Life will get better, trust me. I have endured more pain in thirty years than most people endure in a lifetime and I am still standing. Most of the bullying I dealt with was emotional. It is only by the grace of Jesus Christ that I SURVIVED!

A special dedication to my little sisters: Biancca Ollina Ball (15) and Davina Dorothy Parks (7). Biancca is a true leader who has an outstanding yet goofy personality. She wears her heart on her sleeve and will go above and beyond for anyone just like me. Davina may come off as a bossy leader, but she just has a very strong opinionated personality. She has a big heart as well, but she keeps it covered with many layers. One may think she does not have one, but she does. It takes a while to see it. They are two young leaders who will help improve and empower the world as they get older. I love you with every breath in my body and every inch of my soul. I will always be here for you no matter what! KISSES☺

New International Version
Reckless words pierce like a sword, but the tongue of the wise brings healing. Proverbs 12:18
Blessed is the man who finds wisdom, the man who gains understanding. Proverbs 3:13

Table of Contents

PART I: CHILDHOOD AND ADOLESCENT EXPERIENCES

CHAPTER ONE

First Grade

Boys use physical intimidation tactics to enforce bullying.

My parents were going through a divorce and my siblings and I had to live with our maternal grandparents. Paw Paw and granny raised us the best way they knew how. The clothes we wore were not as good as the other kids. My classmates always teased and picked on me because of the clothes I wore. My mother attended a Pentecostal church regularly before the divorce. Therefore, the women wore dresses all the time, which is why we wore dresses all the time. The kids use to ask just about every day why I wore dresses all the time. They were very mean. When I turned five my classmates called me "sainty fide-five." I also had a bad skin condition that affected my legs and arms, but mostly my legs. If something bit me or I scratched myself, the results left a very dark spot on my body and it took a long time to heal.

My first grade teacher was Mrs. Puckett. She was white and average height for a woman. She had short curly, golden brown hair. She wore glasses. She was a strict teacher, but I had no problem with her. The one thing I will always remember about her is her hips. She had a small waist line and some wide hips as well as a big butt. The boys always cracked jokes or pointed at it when she was at the board or bending over helping a student at a desk. The fact that she was strict kept a lot of my classmates from being mean to me. Unfortunately, she could only be at one place at a time. I am not too sure why, but my first and second grade class was in a tan double-wide trailer with a dark brown roof. First grade was on one end and second grade was on the other end. The classes were separated by two bathrooms and a water fountain. The section was closed off by two doors. It was like a bathroom in a college dorm shared by roommates, but bigger. Mrs. Puckett allowed us to have water breaks throughout the day.

One particular day, half of the class was lined up to get water. Mrs. Puckett had to prop the door open and stand there to be able to watch all of us. She made sure the students who were in the classroom were seated and being obedient as well as the students getting water. I do not know what happened that day, but she had to go in the classroom for something. I was with the group getting water and was next in line, but when I stepped up to the water fountain I was pushed. I fell into the wall very hard and bumped my head. My dress flew up.

It was blurry at first as I looked up from the floor, but as my vision became clear I realized it was Melvin standing at the fountain looking down over me. He was an African-American. He was tall with a low haircut. His skin complexion was dark but it was not smooth. He had big hands and long, big feet. Once he finished drinking from the water fountain, he looked at me in the meanest way possible and said, "Next time hurry up and get out the way with your ugly self." There were four other kids behind him. They just stood there and did nothing probably because they were too scared. He was a big bully. No one told on him.

I slowly got up, dusted myself off and got at the end of the line to get water. As I stepped up to drink from the fountain, tears began to develop in my eyes. I tried to hold them back, but one slowly rolled down my left cheek. I quickly wiped it, got water, and went back to my seat. In music class one day, he pulled my dress up while I was sitting in the chair. He sat behind me and had pulled my dress up as soon as I sat down. It had been up the entire class time and all the other kids were laughing at me.

I am not too sure what happened to Melvin, but when I went to the second grade he did not come back. I think he moved to another town. I just remember feeling good that he was no longer at Greenlee Elementary. He used to call me "Spot." He said I had black spots on my legs like a white dog with spots. He whistled during recess, on our way to lunch, or sometimes during class and say, "Come here Spot. Here girl!" He patted his leg as he whistled.

CHAPTER TWO

Second Grade

Bullying is a way of getting what one wants through coercion or force. It is a way for someone to establish perceived superiority over another person.

During recess one day I had no one to play with, which was a common thing. The girls in my class did not care to play with me. I was a tomboy and I played with the boys most of the time. Even then I did not care to gossip or allow myself to be around gossipers, which was probably why I did not hang around a bunch of girls or shall I say Jesus did not allow them to be around me. Thank You!!! Anyway, during recess I was all alone for some reason I did not want to play with the boys that day. The girls were in huddles as usual either playing some sort of hand game or trying to get the boys attention. I felt very alone that day. By then I was wearing pants because my grandmother decided to let us wear pants. She either sewed them or got them from some of her friends, "hand me downs." I was just glad to be wearing pants. I was playing on the monkey bars the two parallel kind. They were silver and metal. Some kind of way I positioned myself on top of the bars like the gymnastics do. The next thing I knew someone came by, hit my leg and I fell. My legs split as I came down right on my vagina. I did not even go tell the teacher. I slowly got up and walked toward the building. I stood there until the bell rung. I had a bruise for about a week.

I was extremely close to my second grade teacher. Her name was Mrs. Buckner and she was Caucasian. She always had an enthusiastic personality. She was mean as well, but of course me being a teacher now, I understand why she was "mean." Mrs. Gilliam was African-American. She could be just as "mean" at times. Mrs. Buckner and Mrs. Gilliam were great teachers. They were both short and always smiling. Mrs. Buckner was the head teacher. Mrs. Gilliam was the assistant teacher. The one thing I will never forget about them was how well they worked together. They were authoritative. If one of us needed to talk to them about anything, we knew that we could. We also knew our boundaries and the consequences we would face if we were disobedient.

A parent surprised one of my classmates with a birthday party one Friday afternoon. His name was Dennis. He was tall and Caucasian with the prettiest brownish curly hair. He was skinny and of course he grew well into his body as we got older. He was fine to me! I always had a crush on him. His mom, Mrs. Buckner, and Mrs. Gilliam passed out the cake and ice cream. His mom had these pretty little race car plates and napkins. They were white, trimmed in green with a black racecar in the middle with matching napkins.

I was waiting in line to get my plate. I was standing behind Chloe Hall. She was short and Caucasian with very long black hair. I always thought she was biracial because her skin was slightly darker than most kids her race. Adam was standing behind me." Adam was a little taller than I was. He was an African-American with a low top fade haircut. His skin complexion was a caramel. He joined our class in second grade. He came from another school.

As I moved up in line he was talking about me to his boys who were behind me. He said, "I'm gonna tell my mom to throw me a party like this one on my birthday. It's going to be better than this one though." He always had something negative to say. No matter how good something was, he always saw the negative in it. He continued to say, "Man I wonder who else mom will throw a party. I like eating ice cream and cake. We know who ain't going to have a birthday party. Ketta! Her mom doesn't ever come up here. She lives with her grandparents. They drive that raggedy ass tan car." Everyone who heard burst out laughing. He kicked me on the back of my heel. Then he took the tip of his foot and held down the back of my shoe. My shoe came off of my foot. The class laughed even louder. I did not say anything to Adam when he made all of those comments. The fact of the matter was that he was right. I was sad for the rest of the day.

Mrs. Buckner came over as soon as she heard all of the noise. I never even turned around to look at Adam or defend myself. After I fixed my shoe, I dropped my head as I moved forward in line. Mrs. Buckner was furious because the class was being disrespectful and laughing loudly. She went directly to Adam. He always got in trouble and if ever there was commotion, he was the cause of it. She said, "If you do not stop misbehaving, you will not get any ice cream or cake. You will also lose your recess time next week!" There was complete silence.

She was the kind of teacher who always paid attention to EVERYONE no matter how busy she was. She pulled me to the side and asked, "What happened Laketta? Who was picking on you? Was it Adam?" I just stood there looking at the floor like I had just lost my best friend. I said nothing. She walked me back over to the line. I knew not to tell because I would probably get beat up or picked on for a few weeks. She moved Adam to the end of the line, but he made sure I got his message. He softly said, "If you told on me, you are gonna get it. I will get someone to beat you up, if I don't do it myself." When I got on the bus, I sat on the front seat behind the bus driver. I looked out the window and quietly cried all the way home.

CHAPTER THREE

Third Grade

*Bullying is a form of intimidation or domination toward
someone who is **perceived** as being weaker.*

Third grade was when the bullying began to get extremely worse. I met the meanest person and a long time bully, Leon. He was average height for a boy his age. His complexion was smooth and brown like the color of a paper bag. He was every girl's dream boyfriend. He kept his hair cut in a low top Lil' Boosie fade. He wore the tightest and freshest clothes. He was clean every day from head to toe. He had an outgoing personality. He was not the smartest in the class or shall I say he only did what he had to in order to get by. Actually, he failed the third grade and that is how he ended up in our class until we graduated high school.

He possessed traits of a leader, but of course he did know it at that moment. All the boys wanted to be him and have what he had. Therefore, those who hung around him did what he did no matter how it made others feel or the consequences they faced for being disobedient. He was the youngest of his family. His older brothers were handsome as well. They all were athletic, especially in football. He was sneaky and very mischevious. He was very manipulating. He always got others to do his dirty work. If by chance he was disobedient and got caught, he blamed it on someone else or made sure he took someone down with him.

Mrs. Anderson was my third grade teacher. She was very strict. She was not a favorite teacher of mine. I was a good kid, but teachers who are authoritarian just teach and enforce discipline. Therefore, they do not pay attention to other issues students may be going through. If they do notice any change in a student they usually ignore it and keep teaching.

I was standing in line during recess waiting to buy some laffy taffy candy. I loved the banana flavor. Due to the fact that my grandparents were raising us, my siblings and I did not always get money to buy snacks during recess every day. Therefore, anytime we did I was excited. At that time the snacks were in a small room next to the principal, Mr. Mortin's office. The room was brown inside. The walls were made of the material that looks like wood, but like a thin sheet of plywood. There were two tables. The line always stretched outside the door into the hallway. One table had a big box full of a variety of chips. The other table had all the candy on it. There was a teacher standing at the end waiting to collect money. The money box was rusted silver with one big slot for cash and five different small slots for change.

I finally made it inside the room. I was excited and just felt okay that day. Then all of a sudden someone fell into my back. I was very shy then and my self-esteem was very low. I thought I was the ugliest person in the world. I heard one of my classmates, a boy, say "Do it again. She not gonna do anything cause she scared!!!" Of course I was pushed again. I ended up bumping the girl in front of me who just happened to be Karina. Karina had a dark skin complexion. She was the baby and only girl of her family.

She did not have much hair on her head either. She was short and pigeon toed. She was quiet and sneaky. She was mean and stayed in trouble, but mainly for fights. She failed the third grade and was a bully. Everyone was scared of her. The only girls who hung out with her were the ones who wanted to "fit in" or "belong" to a click. Karina got mad of course. She pushed me back hard. I did not do anything, but stand there and take it. I have always been a lover and not a fighter.

Mrs. Anderson came over once she noticed all the commotion. She never asked questions about anything. She just punished whomever she saw. Karrina and I had to miss out on recess for three days. As we sat in our desk, Karrina kept whispering she was going to beat me up for getting her in trouble. The next couple of weeks I remained up under any teacher I seen to avoid her. I stayed in class during recess pretending to finish classwork. I asked if I could help clean up the classroom. During lunch I sat as close to the teachers as I could. As days passed, she eventually forgot about wanting to beat my butt.

My mom combed Ardeshia and my hair for the week. She braided it real pretty or put beads on it so granny would not have anything to do, but wake us up and get dressed to get on the bus. That is really the only times I really remember momma being around. We seen her, but it was for a brief moment. I did not like it when momma went out of town or stayed gone for a long time because that meant granny had to comb our hair. She did the best she could as always, but hair combing was not her thing. The kids at school reminded me of that fact every day.

I got off the bus one Monday beginning the week with granny's hair combing. I almost made it through the day without anyone being mean to me until Mrs. Anderson took us to the cafeteria to eat lunch. After I got my tray, I sat down with my class to eat. Mrs. Buckner was escorting her class out of the cafeteria. She always spoke to me after I left her class no matter where I was or what I was doing. She walked down the aisle beside the table my class was sitting at. When she made it to me, she knelt down and said, "Hey Laketta. Are you making good grades and behaving in class." I gladly responded, "Hi Mrs. Buckner. Yes ma'am I'm still making good grades and being good." As she stood upright and proceeded to go to her class, she noticed my hair and said, "Your mom is out of town huh?" I said, "Yes ma'am. I knew she did not mean anything by that statement. It felt good to see that she remembered me telling her when I was in her class that when my hair looked like Celie from *The Color Purple*, my mom was out of town and granny had to comb it.

Almost everyone at my table started laughing and whispering about my hair and at what Mrs. Buckner said. Leon took it to the extreme. He picked at me for the rest of the day. In fact, he was mean for the remainder of the week. He would say things like, "Well ya'll Ketta momma out of town. Her granny combed her hair ugly as usual. That is why she don't have a boyfriend and none of the girls play with her. She already ugly and that hair style make her uglier." I did not even go outside for recess the remainder of the week. I did all that I could to stay in the building in the classroom. I helped clean the classroom or assisted with paperwork.

The only good times I felt free and when no one really bothered me was during physical education class. Mr. Atkinson was the teacher. He was Caucasian and very tall. His hair was sandy red. He had a thick beard. Sometimes he let it get a little long to where it hung over his top lip just a little. When he talked, a few of the hairs that hung over his lip moved. ⊠ He was a clean cut man. He also taught Math. He was an authoritative teacher. He went over the classroom rules on the first day of school and he did not have to reinforce them much throughout the school year. Everyone took him serious. He was a great PE teacher. He introduced a variety of activities every year. He was there the entire time I was at Greenlee Elementary.

When he first seen me he knew exactly who my mom was. He said, "Is your mother Veronica Elliott?" I told him yes. That was a good day because he said that in front of the class as he was calling roll. The other kids were jealous and wanted him to remember their parents, but he did not. They were nice to me that day as well. I was very active and played every sport that I could. I absolutely loved BASKETBALL. During PE class, if we were allowed to choose players for our team, I was always chosen in the top five. Everyone was always glad to have me on their team. Sometimes Mr. Atkinson lined the class up on the wall. He walked down the line and gave use numbers. Then he said, "If your number is 1 go to that end. If your number is 2, go to that end…" He continued telling us where to go until all the groups were sectioned off. If my team won or was successful in whatever activity Mr. Atkinson had us doing I was on top of the world. No one bullied me on days like that.

CHAPTER FOUR

Fourth Grade

*Hundreds of children stay home from school
because of fearing they will get bullied.*

I began to have crushes on boys and just like any other little girl I wanted a boyfriend. I had the biggest crush on Leon. Yes, the boy who bullied me. He was just fine to me, very popular, and bad. What good girl does not like bad boys? Of course he only paid attention to the pretty, flawless, popular girls. It is amazing how stupid boys are at that age. When my classmates found out I had a crush on him they were mean about it. During recess or lunch they said, "Leon got a new girlfriend Laketta." Leon looked toward me and loudly said, "That ugly girl will never be my girlfriend!" After saying that, he threw something at me or tripped me as I was walked up the aisle to turn my class work or homework in. I did end up getting a boyfriend. Actually, I had two boys who liked me. I went with them at different times of course. Their names were Tyree and Kendrick.

Tyree was older because he failed the fourth grade as I was promoted to the fourth grade. He was African-American. His skin complexion was smooth and the color of honey. He kept a low fade haircut. He had fly gear to wear to school. He came from a good family. He lived with his grandmother who raised him the best way she could. His family was stable and wealthy. His grandmother owned a corner store. I saw it every day on my bus ride home. He was a troublemaker, but not in a bad way. He was more of a class clown. He did stupid things just to make us laugh. He was very successful at it too. Peer pressure is a serious thing. Tyree cared about what his boys thought, he wrote me one of those letters saying, "Will you go with me? Circle yes or no." He gave it to one of the girls and they gave it to me. I circled yes of course and passed it back to him. The hurtful thing was that in public I had to act like we were not together. I was too ugly I guess. He did not want to get picked on by his boys. He eventually broke up with me once everyone found out we were a couple. I was hurt to the core. I never let anyone see me cry, but when I got home I went to my room and cried my eyes out.

Kendrick was more of the quiet, shy type. He came from a good family. His dad was and still is a preacher. He always dressed nice and matched from head to toe. Surprisingly, he got picked on a lot mostly by Leon who was supposedly his best friend. Kendrick, also known as "Dino," had a nice neat high top fade. He was short with a brown complexion like Denzel Washington's. His front teeth were big, white and beautiful.

He was very sensitive and emotional. He cried when his feelings were hurt. The boys constantly picked on him because of that. Whenever they were joking around they said, "Yall better leave Dino alone before he start crying like he always do!" Some kind of way he and I were attracted to each other. He wrote me a letter asking me to go with him. He was left-handed with great penmanship. He wrote very nice and neat. When he wrote me letters they were long and detailed. He did not say stupid childish things like the rest of the boys. He wrote me poems also. The only thing I did not like about him was the fact that we had to keep our relationship a secret because the class would pick on him for being with an ugly, unpopular girl. We dated on and off until the seventh grade. He also made good grades.

As far as the girls to hang out and be friends with, there were none. There were three girls: Natasha, Libby, and Dayanna. All the girls were African-American. Natasha was average in weight and height; well she was a little juicy. She had pretty brown skin. She had shoulder length hair. Of the three, she was the nicest and most respectful. She bit her nails a lot and sucked her thumb, which was why her top stuck out of her mouth a little.

Libby was very dark and a little overweight. Her skin complexion was dark brown. She had the biggest dimples when she smiled as well as beautiful teeth. She was more noticeable than the other two. She did anything to get attention. She laughed at any and everything. She had shoulder length hair as well. She loved boys and they gave her all the attention she could handle and more.

Dayanna was the shy one. She was quiet as well. Her hair was very, very short. She was very skinny and tall. Her skin complexion was caramel or one could even say "red." She wore glasses. She bit her nails as well. Natasha and Libby came from a stable nuclear family. Dayanna was raised in a single-parent home with her mom.

Of all the girls to hang with, I wanted to belong in their click. All they did was dress nice, laugh, and talk about people in a silly way. They laughed and talk about me a lot, especially Libby. She was the ring leader. Dayanna was more of a follower. All three of them had older sisters who were somewhat around the same age. I use to always ask Jesus why I did not have an older sibling, a brother preferably to really protect me. As a matter of fact, I think I was the only one in my class who was the oldest.

There was another click that kept up a lot of drama and instigated fights as well as beat others up. The click included Frida and Karina. Frida's skin complexion was dark. She was average height and very skinny. She did not have much hair on her head. One of her teeth were missing in the front at the top. The fact that the tooth was missing made the tooth next to it look very big. Sometimes it looked as if it was going to pop out through her lips. She stayed in trouble because of her mouth. She talked in class during lecture all the time. She talked about everybody. She stayed in fights. She was the second oldest girl of nine, at the moment, kids! Karina was still very much the same, but had a jerry curl.

They both missed a lot recess time due to their disobedience. There were about three more girls in their click, but their names do not stick out like those two. They were all flunkies. Our class picked Frida up in the fourth grade. They probably were the biggest bullies. Strangely, everybody wanted to be around those two probably because they were scared of them and figured if they hung with them, they would not beat them up or just to belong to a "bad" click. Either way they were horrible. They tortured me from the fourth grade up to the seventh grade.

I was playing on the merry-go-round during recess one day. There were two other kids on there with me. Frida and Karina came over and called a few boys over as well. I rarely got on the merry-go-round because I would get really sick if it went to fast. I could control my own pace when I played on it alone. They began to spend it extremely fast. The more I asked them to stop the faster they pushed it. My foot ended up getting caught under it some kind of way. It threw me a few feet and I landed hard. I was dusty and skinned up from head to toe.

A teacher eventually came over and broke the crowd up. She helped me up and asked who did it repeatedly. At first I was not even focused on what she was saying because I was hurt, embarrassed, and tortured once again without defending myself. When I finally focused on what she was asking I told her I did not know. I was not stupid. I knew if I told who was responsible for what happened that I would get beat up. Whenever things like that happened to me I just prayed and cried. I prayed more for them than I did myself.

There were two boys: Marco and Lamar, who rode my bus and bullied me as well. They were African-American. It is amazing how boys have a stupid way of showing that they like a girl around that age. Lamar had a dark skin complexion, was overweight, and short. Marco was actually cute. He had a caramel complexion and was average height for his age. He was a little muscular with a low top fade, light brown eyes and big lips. He was a part of a big family. There were at least ten siblings who all lived in a small trailer with their mom. I am not too sure if he had failed a grade or not, but Lamar was in his right grade.

For at least about three weeks those two just would not leave me alone. The bothered me on the bus, during recess, and especially when the bell rung and school was dismissed. I could not enjoy myself during recess or on the bus. The bus ride was probably the worst because it was at least an hour long. I was the first to get on and the last to get off every day. They got off right before me. Mr. Prescott did not allow any moving on the bus. He was very strict, but some kind of way Marco still ended up close to where I sat if not directly on my seat. He pulled my hair, told me I was ugly, and hit me. Then it changed, he started asking me to be his girlfriend and rubbing on me in a sexual way. I did not like the situation either way. Lamar did not really bother me on the bus. He really only did it because Marco influenced him to. All Lamar did was trap me in a corner in the hallway or by the trees outside while they both rubbed and touched me in sexual ways. It all came to a stop when the bell rung one afternoon to get on the bus.

Mrs. Bright, a Caucasian teacher, and my all-time favorite teacher, was on duty that week. She was an authoritative. She was very tall. She had wide hips and thighs. Her waist line was small and her stomach was flat. Her hair was cut short in a bob style. She was a brunette. Marco and Lamar hid on the side of the building and waited for me to walk by. They did that daily for at least two weeks. One day I got up the courage to tell Mrs. Bright about them. I did not go into detail about everything. I just told her they got on my nerves and bothered me a lot. I think that was the first time I ever felt protected and safe. She asked me where they were. I took her to the side of the building and sure enough they were there.

When they saw her, their eyes got big. I could tell they were scared because they knew they were in trouble. Mrs. Bright made them apologize. She asked them what I did to cause them to treat me that way. It was amazing because neither one of them could respond. Even though children were running and being loud trying to get to their bus, for a moment it felt as though time had stopped and it was just us four standing there. They were so quiet and ashamed that one could hear a pin drop! She made them get on the bus. They ran as if someone was chasing them. She walked me to the bus. Once I got to my seat I stuck my hand out the window and waved good-bye to her. Surprisingly, I had no more trouble out of those two.

CHAPTER FIVE

Fifth Grade

Physical bullying is the most obvious form of bullying. The instigator attempts to physically dominate another person. It includes kicking, punching, or any other physically harmful activities intended to put fear in a person.

I was still a tomboy, but I began to want to really fit in and belong. I attempted many times to dress and carry myself like a young lady, but evidently I was not successful. I wore some light blue casual pants and a pretty black shirt with colorful designs on it. By then my mom had put a jerry curl in my hair. I wanted it because I was getting older and pony tails were for little girls. I kept it shaved in the back and had the rest kind of short in a bob cut.

I got off the bus and walked down the hall to class. As I walked in no one really said anything, but I could feel the stares and hear the whispering. It came time to go to lunch. Mrs. York took us to lunch. She was our history teacher. She was an African-American. She was old. She had long gray hair. She was short. She had a big butt and wide hips. Her waist line was small. She had no stomach either. She wore glasses from time to time. They were reading glasses because she only put them on when grading papers or reading. Most of the time she had them in her hand or hanging out the side of her mouth. ☺

Her style of teaching was all over the place. I did learn some things in her class, but she was just very unorganized. The kids knew it too. She had no control over her class. She put our assignments on the board and sat down. We had to define vocabulary words for the chapter. Once we finished, she called on names to read out loud in class. There was nothing wrong with that. It was however, something wrong with how she went about doing it. There was one unusual thing she did that most teachers did not do back then. She did not sit at her desk. Instead, she put a chair in front of the classroom, a few inches from the chalk board, and sat there with a stack of papers and books on her lap. As we read, she sat there with her glasses on the tip of her nose. If someone made a sound or was being disobedient, she did not lift her head. She looked out of the top of those glasses. ☺ Her desk had a lot of stuff all over it.

She took us to lunch every day during fourth period. We lined up in the hallway as usual. As we were walking to the cafeteria of course Leon had to initiate something. This time it was different attention. I do not quite remember who was standing behind me, but he was at least two people behind me. I heard him say, "I dare you to touch it!" A few seconds after that I felt a hand rub and grab my butt. I did not do or say anything because I could not believe it. I was excited, felt pretty and wanted it for a minute. I cannot remember who that was that touched me, but once they seen I was not going to stop them, they continued to do it. Surprisingly, Leon began to grab and rub my butt. Even though he treated me like crap, I still had a huge crush on him. I wanted him to like me the way he liked other girls. He continued to touch me until I sat down to eat. I could hear him and his crew whispering about me at the lunch table. I was a very intelligent girl who knew exactly what they were probably saying, but I wanted to enjoy the spotlight for a minute.

Once the class finished lunch, we headed back to our class. Mrs. York always allowed us to get water or go to the bathroom. Leon had of course spread the word about touching me. All the other boys wanted a feel as well. They cornered me some kind of way in the hall. I was looking and moving around trying to escape, but I could not. It was a circle of about six boys with me in the middle. I was like a bouncing ball going from one to the next, but each time I moved they would grab my butt, vagina, and breasts. It was then when I realized I did not want the attention all the other girls had been getting!

I eventually made it to class. For the rest of the day I was tortured emotionally by Leon and Brandon Butler. Brandon was another flunky. He was Lamar's older brother. He was tall and stocky with a big head. He looked mean and intimidating. His skin complexion was dark. His butt was big and high on his back. One of his front teeth was chipped. Leon made it known that I was scared to do anything with boys. I did not defend myself at all as he spread those hideous rumors. He said, "I don't know what I was thinking anyway cause she still ugly, has no ass, got spots on her legs, and dark circles around her eyes!" After all of that I rarely wore clothes that revealed the actual curves of my body. I had always worn big clothes that covered my body, but I continued to for a long time after that.

The playground area was big. It was in front of the school when I was in the first and second grade, but was later moved to the back of the school in a more grassy area. There was a big "lake" so to speak at the back of the playground. I later learned it was where the urine and digestive products of our bodies went once the toilet was flushed. It had a huge fence around it to keep the children away. The monkey bars, which I liked because no rarely played on them, were placed a few yards on the side of the "lake." The parallel silver bars were immediately beside the monkey bars. A small swing set of four was a few feet in front of the silver bars. I did not like those much because the seats were rectangular and square. The seesaws were next to the small swing set. The merry-go-round was next to the small swing set. In front of the merry-go-round was the huge swing set with at least eight to ten swings on it. Everyone loved the merry-go-round and the big swing set.

The seats were soft and flexible. On the side of the big swing was a big open area with small trees. Most of the time girls were on that side gossiping, kissing boys, or hiding from the teachers.

Basketball goals were installed on the playground on the side where the "lake" was. There was a lot of open field on that side as well. The boys played football over there. I was very excited because basketball was my life. I brought my basketball every day. That was the only way we could play. The school did not provide a basketball. For a while I felt okay going to school. Everyone was nice to me, but only because I had a basketball and they wanted to play with it. It was mostly boys. The only girls who played were Karina and I. I was not stupid meaning I was well aware of the fact that they only reason they were being nice to me was because they wanted to play with my ball. I used that ball as my leverage. I had no problem telling them, "As long as ya'll let me play, WE can use MY ball." After a few days of playing with the boys, I realized I was not having fun anymore. I was on the court true enough. They passed the ball to me and I took a couple of shots, but gradually it was as if I was not even on the court.

Eventually, I stopped bringing my ball to play because when I set foot on the court I wanted to play! One day during recess, I did not play. Instead I walked around dribbling my ball. I had good ball handling and passing skills. I ended up where a group of boys were playing football. I decided I wanted to play. I stood there until one of them noticed me. It took a while and I began to think they were not going to ask me. I dropped my head and turned to walk away. Then I heard, "Hey Ketta come back and let us play with your ball. Ours tore up." I am not too sure what happened to the football they had, but they wanted to play football with my basketball.

I went back and we played football with my ball. Everything was going just fine. Then all of a sudden I had the ball running toward the end zone and BOOM! It felt like I had run into a brick wall only it was Leon. We were playing "touch," but when I got the ball he tackled me to the ground. I have been claustrophobic ever since. He was smothering me. He said, "Hey ya'll come pile on." The boys came running and jumped on me. They did not know I was beneath the pile. They just did what Leon said. I felt as if I was about to die. All I seen was darkness and it felt like I was walking through a dark tunnel and I was never going to get to the end and see the light. (I have been claustrophobic ever since.) I still had my ball. Finally, they began to get off of me. I slowly got up and walked away. I was very sore. I went to the side of the building and cried. I did not understand why Leon was that cruel, especially to me. He really did not like me.

Keiona was my cousin and she was older than me. She failed the sixth grade. She rode the bus with me. As I stated earlier we did not have a lot of income coming in, but we survived. I do not ever remember my momma telling us we could not get anything. We did not ask for much, but whenever we did ask for something she always found a way to get it for us. We did not wear name brand clothing or shoes, but one evening when I got off the bus momma told me she was going to buy me a pair of reeboks. She asked what color I wanted and I said black. Something told me not to tell anyone because she may not get them, but I was excited about finally fitting in and having a pair of name brand shoes like my classmates. Momma had informed me at least a week ahead of time about buying the shoes. I began to slowly tell everyone about me "supposedly" getting some reeboks. I especially told Keiona.

I got home on Thursday and sure enough momma bought me some black high top shoes, but they were not reeboks. Instead they were some knock off black high top "hoop" shoes. I got on the bus Friday morning and wore them proudly, but I knew Keiona was going to say something. Once she got on the bus and seen those shoes she said,"Ya'll look at Ketta new "Reeboks" Veronica bought her!" And if that was not enough once we got off the bus and was walking to class she yelled the same thing in the hallway. Everyone was picking on me and laughing. From that moment on, if I was told I was going to get something or someone was going to do something for me, I kept it to myself!

Fifth grade was when I had my first fight. I have only been in two fights my entire life. Some gossip started one day that involved Frida. My name got caught in the middle some kind of way. I was in a particularly good mood that day because I had a new outfit on and a new necklace my aunt Sandy bought me. It was some dark brown corduroy pants and a pretty dark, short sleeve shirt with different colors and designs on it. By the time we went to lunch Frida had already let it be known that she was going to beat me up because I had supposedly "lied" on her. I was nervous and scared, but I prayed to Jesus about the situation.

We went to the bathroom after lunch as usual. The bathroom had pastel green walls. The top half of the wall was lighter than the bottom half. There were at least four stalls. The second one upon entering did not have a door on it. Most of the time no one used it, but if they did another person stood in front as a shield while the other used the bathroom. There were three sinks with two square like mirrors above them. The mirrors were not that big. There was a soap and paper towel dispenser to the right. The windows were high, but it was hard to see out of them. The panes were not clear like most are. They were blurry.

There were a lot of girls in there because they wanted to see a fight. They were instigating and plotting the attack. I went into the stall and used the bathroom as if they were not there. As I was pulling my pants up, the bathroom became silent. I took a deep breath and proceeded to walk out. Frida was standing in my face talking a bunch of crap. I did not say anything. I continued walking toward the sink to wash my hands. The next thing I knew she punched me in the right eye, hard. All I saw was a rainbow of colors in my eye. I reached my hand and arm out to feel for the wall, but all I felt was air. I did not fight back. She grabbed my shirt and slung me to the wall near the sink and mirror. When she noticed I was not fighting back she just stopped and walked out. I got myself together and looked in the mirror. I noticed my necklace was lying on the floor. It was the first piece of jewelry I ever received. I slowly picked it up and walked out of the bathroom. When I walked into class, I acted as if nothing happened. I did not even tell the teacher. I do not know if Frida told them she beat me up or not and actually did not even care.

When I got off the bus that evening I put my book bag down and walked to my aunt Sandy house. She had a yard full of beautiful flowers and no matter what I was going through I could always go there and look at the flowers to get peace. I did not tell her about my day. Instead I just listened to her talk about her flowers as usual. I did not say anything about the necklace either. She had a variety of flowers as well as a variety of colors. She had this white overpass like what couples stand under when they get married. It had a flower vine growing on it. I use to always tell her I was going to get married in her yard. She lit up like a Christmas tree every time I said that.

CHAPTER SIX

Sixth Grade

Emotional bullying is far worse than verbal bullying. It makes a person feel isolated, alone, and depressed.

The bullying I received from this point on was more emotional than physical. Every year the school hosted a Halloween carnival. The main reason people came was to be with their girlfriend or boyfriend and show off to the public how in "love" they were. I of course never had a boyfriend to show off, but this particular year Leon asked me to go as his date. I was excited and could not believe the finest boy in the school wanted me to be his date! My family and I arrived at the carnival around seven. It started around six every year. As soon as I walked inside the gym I was looking for Leon. I could not wait to introduce him to my mom. I knew she would be proud.

When I finally seen Leon, to my surprise he was standing by another girl. It still had not dawned on me what was going on. When he seen me, he walked over to me and these were his words, "When you get a body like that, I will allow you to walk by my side. Look at her ain't she beautiful. She got titties, ass, and a beautiful face." Then he turned and walked away. I caught a glimpse in my peripheral at the boys laughing at what just happened. I watched him walked over to Kenya, put his arm around her neck, and walk away.

It was as if no one was in the room but us three. There I stood on one side of the gym as they were hugged up at center court. The spotlight was on him and me as he whispered earlier in my ear, but the closer he got to Kenya my light faded and theirs got brighter. I do not remember anything else that night. I attempted to play the games and act as if nothing happened. I did the best I could to hold back the tears, but it was too hard. I walked outside in the dark, stood on the side of the building and cried as if someone had died. I cut the tears short when I heard someone coming and went back inside.

The sixth grade class got to go on a field trip to the Jackson Zoo every year. I was excited and looking forward to it. The only thing that bothered me was having enough money to buy stuff with as well as someone to be my friend on the trip. Every time we had field trips most of my classmates always had a lot of money. Their parents made them sandwiches and snacks to take. They had pretty lunch boxes to take as well. Whenever I had lunch to bring, I had to put it in a bag. I got teased and picked on because of that. Not only was I hurt behind that fact, but embarrassed also. My classmates had money to buy souvenirs. Paw Paw, granny, and momma did give me some money, but it was no more than ten dollars. I used that to eat or get something to drink. Sometimes I did not eat because I wanted to be able to buy a souvenir from the gift shop even if it was just an eraser, keychain, or pencil.

It ended up being one of the worst trips ever. I had no friends or boyfriend to walk around with. Libby, Natasha, and Dayanna hung together. Leon, Kendrick, and a few other boys hung together. Donna, Chloe, Dalton, Brady, and Amanda hung together. Everyone was with a teacher walking around the zoo. We got to choose the group we wanted to be a prior to the trip. There was a sheet in our homeroom teacher's room. We signed under what group we wanted to be in. I ended up in Mrs. Bright. ☺ The kids in my group ignored me and did not include me in their conversations as we walked. As we loaded up to get on the bus I knew I was not going to have a good time. I sat toward the front close to teachers. I did not want to be a part of what was going on in the back. They were being loud, rude, disrespectful, and rubbing and touching all over each other. I did not want to be a part of that. I sat next to the window, watch the trees, and looked in the sky the entire trip. I thought, "If I could be any animal in the world, I would like to be a bird. I could travel wherever I wanted without having to pay anything. I would be free of all the pain and humiliation I face walking the earth. I would be close to the sky, which meant I would be closer to Jesus!"

Once we made it to the zoo there were many other schools as well. Everyone was happy and overflowing with joy. We got off the bus and formed a single-file line. Mr. Atkinson said, "Find your group teacher and go stand beside them. You are to stay with your teacher and group at all times." I immediately ran to Mrs. Bright. Most of the girls wanted to be in her group. She was cool after getting to know her.

As we entered in the zoo I started feeling extremely down. There was a building to the left as I entered. It was the gift shop and where people paid to visit the zoo. I thought, "I know I won't go in there because I do not have enough money to buy anything." Boyfriends and girlfriends were together, best-friends were together. No one tortured me that day, but no one hung around me either. I felt like I was the only person at the zoo and no one else was there. At one point I stood by a fence of the giraffe cage. There were a ton of teachers and children around, yet I felt like I was on a deserted island left to die ALONE. The sun was beaming. I was hot and ready to go.

After almost completing the tour, we came to a fun town area of the zoo. It was like a haunted house only it had snake in glass, spiders in glass, butterflies and other insects in glass windows, and birds walking around. I enjoyed that part. Mrs. Bright asked us questions about the animals and insects as we approached each window. After leaving that section we came to a tunnel and a door. They both lead to the outside, but the tunnel led to a ground hog field. It was a bunch of dirt with holes in it. It was covered with a glass top. As you walked through the tunnel there were four spaced out areas where you could stick your head in and get a closer look at the ground hogs. We were excited about that. We could not wait to get to stick our head in. The teachers and kids were standing outside watching and waving as we put our head in the space.

I was at the back of the group because I did not feel like fighting to go first. I finally got to a space. I put my head in only to realize there was no one out there to see me or take a picture. I looked around to find the ground hogs. When I found them I said, "Well at least ya'll go to see me." I slowly exited the tunnel with tears in my eyes. There was a bunch of ropes at the end of the tunnel. One set was shaped like a spider's web, but it was moveable like a swing. A bunch of kids were on it taking pictures and swinging. The other set was shaped like a big square with miniature squares inside. The square was stationary. The kids walked across it. Beneath the ropes was tree bark. It appeared to be the kind that could be purchased in a Home Depot. It was light brown and pretty.

Once I left the tunnel I walked across the pavement to the gift store. It was getting time to go. Everyone was either sitting or standing with their teacher until others made it out of the tunnel. I wanted to go in the gift store, but decided against that. I was not going to be able to get anything anyway so why go in. In front of the gift store was a few picnic tables made of concrete. There was also a long bench that was made of concrete on the other side of the tables. It was long and we sat on it. I sat by myself and wondered, "If I went missing, would they realize I was gone?" I had no friends and all I wanted to know was, "Why no one wanted to hang around *me*?"

Finally, it was time to go. We formed a single-file line with our group teacher and walked to the home. The ride was exciting for my classmates because the atmosphere was relaxed. The teachers were not fussing at us and it was the last trip before graduating and moving on to the high school. We were no longer little kids anymore. Couples were sitting together, hugged up and sneaking a kiss when they could. The boys were touching on the girls butt, at least the girls who let them. There was someone sitting with me. I do not know who it was, but they moved to another seat with their buddy. That was fine by me because I wanted to be alone and have my seat all to myself. I propped my feet up on the seat, closed my eyes, and laid my head on the seat as I sat upright until we made it back to the school.

CHAPTER SEVEN

Seventh Grade

Girls use verbal and emotional tactics to enforce bullying.

I was excited about the seventh grade just like all my other classmates. We had graduated from Greenlee and were officially at Ethel High School, which was seventh through twelfth grade. Seventh and eighth grade was considered junior high. Ninth through twelfth was high school. I got off the bus and felt like a different person. I was still ashamed of my body and had low self-esteem. I did not wear shorts too often from the second grade to the tenth grade. The only time I wore them was during basketball, softball, or track practice. I had on a short outfit the first day though. It was white with green and pink vertical stripes.

The one thing I was the most excited about in terms of going to Ethel was playing basketball. It was the only thing, besides writing, that took my mind off all the bad things that were going on in my life. I was good at it too. Coach Isaiah Johnson, God rest his soul, was my coach. He had coached at the school for years. He knew an athlete could play or at least should have the potential based on their last name. During tryouts he asked, "Is your mom's name Veronica Elliott?" I was scared and nervous, but I managed to swallow and say, "Yes sir." He also named a few of my aunts and uncles on my dad side who played for him as well. He was a living legend. He coached the girls and boys team, both junior high and high school. He called me into his office one day and asked how I felt about playing on the high school team. I was excited and more honored than anything. Little did I know what I was about to face.

Most of the bullying I dealt with in the seventh grade came from the basketball team. I later on found out that one of the main reasons Coach Johnson moved me up was because most of his starters were on academic probation. They could not play a single game until after Christmas. The main two and leading scores were Lydia and DaShay.

DaShay was a forward. Actually, she played every position. She was just that good. Her skin complexion was caramel. She was very tall and skinny. She had long legs and long arms. She kept her hair cut short. One thing that always stuck out in terms of her appearance was the fact that she had dark eyebrows. She was quiet and kept to herself until she got on the court.

Lydia was a shooting guard. She was a little taller than most of the girls. Her skin complexion was a pretty smooth brown. She was beautiful. She was very outgoing. Everyone loved being around her. The boys wanted to date her and the girls wanted to be her friend. She had a jerry curl. The top was short and the back was shaved nice and neat. She was a girly girl, but when it came time to play ball she hustled. She had a lot of curves on her body. They were Coach Johnson's favorite players. They were also the ones who treated me so bad to the point where I lost interest in playing basketball.

I was the first one to get to the locker room, but I would be the last one to get on the floor because I was ashamed of my body. I did not want the other girls to see me get dressed for fear they would laugh and talk about me just like everyone else did already. One day we were learning some new plays as well as defense. Coach Johnson was a defensive coach. We spent most of practice going over full court presses and zone defenses. On this particular day we were playing man to man, which I grew to despise because it was just too much running and movement. Those girls tortured me to death that day.

We were running a simple box man to man formation. When the point guard brought the ball down the floor, the forwards screened down on the defender to free their teammate who was usually a guard. DaShay came down and screened me hard in my stomach and she held the screen longer than she was supposed to. My stomach and side was bruised up for at least a week!!! When we had a water break I heard her telling the rest of the team, "I'm killing Ketta with those screens."

From that moment on I did not play defense that well because I was scared to. I caught hell from Coach Johnson for years because of my lack of defense. I cried my eyes out in the locker room that day. Basketball practice was my last class of the day. When I got on the bus, I sat next to the window and cried all the way home. To make matters worse Lydia rode my bus and I heard her telling others how they tortured me. The only person on the team the following two years who was nice to me was Charlotte. She was a Caucasian girl who could shoot the lights out of the ball. She wore green contacts and had long blonde hair. Her body was shaped like that of a black girl.

There was a tournament in Kosciusko, Mississippi. It was three days. Even though most of the starters could not play they always dressed out in uniform every game. I started that particular game, which was my first time. I was nervous as I don't know what. It was tradition for the starters to sit on the bench before the game started as the rest of the team stood and listened to Coach Johnson's strategies. As I sat on the bench with the rest of the girls who started I do not remember anything Coach Johnson said, but as we proceeded to stand up and wait for the referees to direct us to the court to position for tip off, I remember hearing Lydia and DaShay say,

"Laketta looks like a ball player. I think she really can hoop. She should do good. We got this game girl." I was excited and nervous at the same time, but my family was there to see me play. I did not want to disappoint Coach Johnson, my team, or my family. They did not come to many of my games.

As the referee stood in the middle of the court and threw the ball up everything felt like slow motion. We got the opening tip. The ball came directly to me! Coach Johnson taught us to set up in the tipoff with the tall and strong forward (5) at center court facing our goal; the small forward (4) in between the three point line and center circle facing the 5; the guards (2 and 3) one on each side of the 5 at center circle on the half court line; and the point guard (1) at the free throw line behind the 5 as a defender.

The five was supposed to hit the ball to the four. The two and three were to sprint toward our goal. Once the four catch the ball, she turned around and quickly passed it to either the two or three, whoever was opened. Most of the time the pass went to the two who was right handed and the quickest. Therefore, she was always on the right side of the five to ensure she made the lay-up!

I dribbled toward our goal, but before I could run a play, I double dribbled and lost the ball. I lost the ball most of the first quarter. Coach Johnson took me out. I was embarrassed more than anything. I knew in my head how I wanted to play and knew I could do it, but for some reason my actions did not show it. I got dressed in the locker room very slow after the game. I did not want to face my family, school, or teammates. We lost of course, but when I made it to where my family was in the bleachers, my Uncle Darren hugged me real tight and told me everything was okay and that I did a good job.

Darren was Sandy's husband and he was the epitome of what I thought every man should be. He was a good husband and most importantly an even better father. When he said that, the tears began to roll fast down my face. He hugged me even harder and told me to stop crying. After a while I did eventually stop crying and enjoyed the rest of the night watching other teams play.

The next week I decided to get up the courage to ask Coach Johnson if I could go back to the junior high team. I knew he would want to know why and I had no clue what I would say. I did not want to tell him how bad the girls were treating me especially Lydia and DaShay. Those two were his favorites. I did not know if he would believe me or if he did I wondered if he would tell them what I said and make matters worse. I eventually talked to him and he gave me this bull crap about him thinking about it. Of course I ended up staying on the high school team. I refused to quit and dealt with it the best way that I could.

The basketball team made it to the championship that year. It was in Bogga Chita, MS. We had to ride the bus almost two hours to get there. Coach Johnson drove the bus as usual, but he had someone to help him. We had hotel rooms and everything. Some of the girls' parents trailed the bus to watch us play. The team consisted of: Shalona (9th), Denisha (9th), DaShay (11th), Lydia (11th), Charlotte (12th), Megan (10th), Francis (10th), Shaunika (9th), Darlene (9th), Yasmine (9th), and myself.

Shalona, Megan, Francis, and Darlene's mothers were chaperones. I remember Shalona's mom especially because she had pretty eyes. Coach Johnson was a big flirt and he most definitely flirted with Ms. Gaines. As I got off the bus I felt alone. The girls had their mothers with them and I did not. It meant the world to me when my parents came to see me participate in extracurricular activities whether it was the Beta Club, Fellowship of Christian Students, Annual Staff, Future Business Leaders of America, Band, basketball, softball, or track. Unfortunately I can count on one hand how many times my parents came to see me. Just that alone ate me up inside.

Most of the girls wanted to be in Shalona's hotel room because her mom was cool. There could only be four girls per room with a chaperone. I did not have anyone on the team that year that liked me or attempted to be my friend. Daisy was my third cousin who lived in my neighborhood and she did not converse with me. Fitting in was more important to her. If the team captains, who were usually juniors and seniors, did not talk to someone on the team no one else did. If they did it was when no one else was around. All of that made my self-esteem go lower and lower.

My interest in basketball began to fade. I still had the desire, but was too intimidated to play from the heart. I did not start anymore games. I rode the bench and when I did get in a game, it was as if I had never seen or touched a basketball in my life. Coach Johnson immediately took me out!

After we got our rooms and unpacked, some of the girls wanted to get in the swimming pool. Coach Johnson said it was okay as long as a parent was out there with us. Shalona, Shaunika, and Denisha persuaded Ms. Gaines to watch them. I did not go for three reasons: I was not invited, I was ashamed of my legs due to my skin condition, and I was terrified of the water in terms of swimming.

My mom did not let us go near swimming pools, beaches, or lakes growing up. When she was young, they went swimming in the Big Black River in West, MS one day. She got stuck in one of those tubes that suck down the water when the river floods. She was submerged under water for almost fifteen minutes. She was sixteen at the time. Every time she tells the story she says, "It felt like something was holding my feet. Then all of a sudden it let me go and I shot out like a cannon ball."

I sat in the hotel room alone and looked out the window as they played in and around the pool. I watched television for a while. Then looked out the window a while. The tears began to roll down my face as I stared out the window. No one even missed me. I heard someone rattling keys at the door. I hurried to sit back on the bed and straighten my face up. I did not let anyone see me cry. It was a parent. She asked, "Why you not outside with the rest of them?" I politely said, "I don't want to. I want to watch TV for a while."

We rested for a while that night and woke up to go to practice at the gym. We played first that night. Once we got dressed in the locker room Coach Johnson came in to give us the pregame talk and strategies. As always his motto was, "Offense wins games, but defense wins championships!" The last thing we did before leaving the locker room was pray. He knelt down on one knee and began to pray:

> "Our father who art in heaven hallowed be thy name. Thy kingdom come, thy will be done, on earth as it is in heaven. Give us this day our daily bread and forgive us our trespasses, as we forgive those who trespass against us. Lead us not into temptation, but deliver us from evil. For thine is the kingdom, the power and the glory forever. Amen." We joined in as he started that prayer every game.

After the prayer we formed a straight line from the shortest player to the tallest. I was the second person in that line until my ninth grade year where I became the first. Yasmine was the first and she ran out with the ball. My heart was beating fast as we waited to run out on the floor. Mrs. Bradley, the assistant coach, gave us the go ahead. We ran out, went to the center of the floor, jogged around the circle at midcourt and went to our end to start the tip drill. Before every game DaShay and Lydia always said, "Ya'll seventh, eighth, and ninth graders better not mess up during drills. We ain't got time to be embarrassed."

I was very intimidated by those two. They were true enough the leading scorers and by far the best players along with Charlotte, but they were just down right evil. If only they had known they were taking a little from me every day! I did not play at all during that game. It was a very close game. DaShay fouled out during the fourth quarter. Coach Johnson looked down the side of the bench and rubbed his head because he had no idea who to put in the game. When he did that, those of us sitting on the sideline did all we could to not make eye contact for fear that he would call on us to get in the game. His always had a calm soothing voice during normal conversation, but during games and sometimes practice, his voice became deep and scary.

After pacing the sideline for a few seconds he yelled, "Daisy let's go!" She jumped up immediately. She was always ready to get in. She had amazing energy. I mean she did not ever seem to get tired. She played as a small forward (4). She was wild and all over the place, but she managed to do her job, which was rebound.

We ended up losing by two points. The team cried once in the locker room. I did not cry. I cried on the bus as we journeyed back to Ethel, but not because we lost. I cried because I did not get to play in an important game and wondered if I had gotten the chance to play would I have I made a difference. I was angry at Coach Johnson for putting me on the high school team for as long as I could remember. He always told me I was lazy, hated running, and could not play defense.

Even though I did not have the attention I wanted from the boys, I still craved having a boyfriend. As usual the boys I wanted did not want me. I had the biggest crushes on Marquise, Samuel, and Jordan. They were all African-American. Marquise and Samuel were "bad boys," thugs so to speak. I loved bad boys. What good girl does not? Jordan was a good boy. All three had bodies to die for: rock hard abs, broad shoulders, noticeable pectorals, strong calves, tear drop quads, and butts made of steel!!!

Marquise had a dark, sexy skin complexion. He changed his hair style a lot. Sometimes he kept it cut low. Sometimes he grew it out and got it braided. He was average height and one hell of an athlete. He was good in every sport. Everyone loved him except for maybe the teachers. He stayed in trouble. He was in fights almost every week. He sold and smoked weed. He was disobedient and talked backed to the teachers. He was a part of the Vice Lord gang. When Lil Wayne first came on the scene as a rapper, Marquise was drawn to him. He even began to refer to himself as "Young Weezy." He always quoted verses or phrases from Lil Wayne's music. Some days he wore big clothes and some days he wore clothes that fit his frame. Regardless of what he wore, he always sagged his pants and wore fresh gear. He carried a red bandanna around with him all day every day. The girls absolutely adored him. The boys wanted to be him.

Samuel had a dark, sexy skin complexion as well. He was a little taller than Marquise. He was an athlete as well, but not well rounded in every sport the way Marquise was. He was very talented in football and track. He was a quiet boy. He was a trouble maker as well, but sneaky with his. He did not get into a lot of fights unless it was necessary. He was respectful to the teachers. He had older brothers. I am quite sure that is where his "bad boy" mentality came from. There were two things that set him apart from the other boys: his hair and his walk. He had long black hair. He kept it braided nice and neat. He was bowlegged. That boy had a sexy walk on him! He sagged his pants, but in a neat way. They fell just below his waist. He wore a belt and always tucked his shirt in, which made it look even neater.

Jordan had a light brown skin complexion. He was short in height. He kept a very low haircut. He was a great athlete, but just like Samuel, not in every sport. He was exceptional in football and track. Of all the boys I had crushes on; he was the only one I seen myself married to. The dream that every young girl has with the perfect husband, four kids, and big house with the white picket fence entered into my thoughts every day I seen him. He wore his clothes nice and neat. Sometimes he sagged. Sometimes he did not. He was very respectful and obedient. He walked on his tip toes, which explained why he had the biggest calves ever. His walk was too cute.

Unfortunately, they only wanted the girls who were having sex or at least made them think they were going to. I was not that kind of girl. On top of that I was nowhere as pretty as the other girls and I was a tomboy!

There was one boy, Christopher, who wanted to be my boyfriend bad. I knew that because everyone reminded me every day. He was not my type for many reasons. He was not attractive and he could just be a mean person. He wore a low top fade just like all the other boys during that time. He was tall and muscular. He dressed okay, but not as good as the other boys. He had an older brother in the eleventh grade. At some point I settled and told him I would be his girlfriend. It was because I wanted to fit in so bad. I wanted to be able to say I had a boyfriend. I wanted someone to walk me to class everyday like the rest of the girls. I wanted to talk on the phone late nights as well, but somewhere down the line it took a turn for the worst.

He started showing signs of possessiveness. I did not like that too well. One night on the phone I broke up with him. I thought he was going to be mad and tell me I was not leaving him. Surprisingly, he was the total opposite. He started crying and begging me to stay with him. I could not believe it!!! That made it easier for me to break up with him. I wanted to fit in of course and as soon as I got off the bus I went to some girls in our grade and told them how Chris cried and begged me not to break up with him. Honestly, I only told one or two girls who I thought I could trust to keep it to themselves. They told the entire class and it got back to Chris.

I was in the hall going to computer class when Chris walked up to me and dissed me. He had me up against the wall. I thought he was going to hit me. He was mad and embarrassed that I told how he acted on the phone. I maintained my composure and did not say or do anything as he pointed his finger in my head and got loud with me. I felt mad and punked in front of everybody. I learned an important lesson that day and that was to not tell people what goes on in my relationships whether good or bad!

CHAPTER EIGHTH

Eighth Grade

Bullying is the most common among middle school children.

The bullying from the eighth grade and up changed because the transition from childhood to adolescence occurred. Peer pressure was very heavy from that point on. Fitting in was the extreme make it or break it stage. There were many different groups to choose from in terms of belonging. Those groups were: 1) the make-up Barbie doll click, 2) the football click, 3) the basketball click, 4) the baseball click 5) the band click, which was broken down into sub-clicks: color guard, flag girls, drum line, horns, clarinets, flutes, etc. 6) the drug head click, 7) the nerd click, and 8) the whore nasty girl click. There were many other clicks to choose from, but those were the major ones. There was one click, which was considered to be at the bottom and that was the "non-belonging" click. Anyone in that click was there because they were not accepted by other clicks or because they were smart enough to understand that one did not have to be a part of a click to be considered important or popular or because Jesus put them there for a reason. I later learned that was the click that I belonged to.

Band was something that I enjoyed as well. I played the flute and was quite good at it. I was either first or second chair in my section out of ten chairs. My section could not stand that fact. Nickie and I began to become friends. She had a twin brother, Nick, whom I adored. My crush on him was not like the other ones. He was not a "bad" boy. He made good grades and played basketball. He was quiet, tall, and a gorgeous dark chocolate thang! They came from a good family.

My self-esteem really began to get low. My clothes got bigger because I was still ashamed of my body. In my mind I was ugly because I had been told that for so long. I did learn something intriguing about myself that year. I had a sense of humor. I was a little comedian who kept those who did hang around me laughing. I did not do it on purpose either. It just flowed naturally. I was the class clown.

I began to notice how teachers treated my classmates based on their popularity, socioeconomic status, and grades. I was a teacher's pet for most of my teachers due to my grades. It is amazing how I maintained A's and B's considering the cards I was dealt. WOW!!! The kids who were popular and came from high income families received special attention. The reason I did not include the "grade" group in the last statement was because not everyone who made good grades came from a high income family. "We" received special attention, but it was very different than the others.

I began to get tortured for making good grades. Most of my teachers called out the top five grades when taking tests, writing papers, or things to that nature. I was blessed to be in the top five most of time. If I was not first with the highest score, I was no or lower than third. I went to a black and white diverse school. From the first grade until graduation from high school I just could not pass Donna, Chloe, or Ronda with grades. They were Caucasian and came from high income families, but they were not snobby or stuck up. They were cool. They made straight A's. The order was usually: Donna, Chloe, Laketta, Ronda. Ronda and I switched places at times.

My classmates tortured me especially the black ones. They said things like, "She got to be the only nigga to act like the white folks and make good grades." It use to hurt my feelings a lot at first, but I later learned that those good grades would get me into a university!" There were times when I felt like I could not win for losing. I still had no boyfriend. In that grade sexual activities were taking place. The boys knew I was not going to do anything. Surprisingly, out of all the bullying and teasing on every issue, sex teasing was not a problem for me. I was proud of myself for having the sense to say NO!

The same three girls whose click I tried to be a part of in the sixth grade were the same three girls I still wanted to hang around: Libby, Natasha, and Dayanna. I was just a tag along whenever they allowed me to be. They could pretty much do whatever they wanted because they had older siblings who were popular, which in turn made them popular.

Patricia was Natasha's and Denisha's older sister. She was a mean big bully. Most kids who hung around her either did so because they were just like her or scared of her. Surprisingly, Natasha was nothing like her. Natasha was a nice person. Everyone wanted to be around her. The boys were crazy about her, especially Tyree.

Libby had an older sister Nichole and older brother, Kamron. Nichole was much older than her. She graduated from Ethel when we were in Greenlee. Kamron was a few years older than her. He was sexy to me. He was quiet and hung out with an okay click of boys who played football. Of course his boys teased him because I had a crush on him. They said things like, "Ah hah, that's why you got an ugly girl who likes you. You can't fuck her because she not giving it up." Kamron never really responded the way most boys did. He softly said, "Man ya'll crazy and wrong for that."

Libby was the total opposite. She was not a bully. She laughed and talked about everybody. She was like a comedian, but one of those D. L. Hugely kind of comedians. She made people laugh by making fun of others. I would just look at her and think to myself, "Why do you have be so mean. Jesus help her." She did all of us like that including Natasha and Dayanna.

Natasha laughed back with her or said something about her. They cracked jokes back and forth on each other. Dayanna was a little more like me. She did not really defend herself or say anything back. We just took the torture and teasing.

The boys were head over heels for Libby. She and Marquise danced around each other until we graduated high school. Marquise was all about sex. He did not interact with any girl unless she was giving "it" up. Libby always asked to go to the bathroom during class, but instead she met up with whomever she was dating at the time and only Jesus knows what they done. It did not take a rocket scientist to figure it out. They boys told anyway. I heard the boys talk about her behind her back. They said things like, "She so stupid with her stanking ass breath. All she can do for me is give me some or suck my dick!"

Dayanna was quiet and kept to herself. Her self-esteem was low as well, but gradually she found herself the older she got. Jewel was her older sister. She was phenomenal in basketball. She graduated when we were in elementary school as well. In a sense, Dayanna did not really have anyone to protect her either. She got picked on and talked about, but not as bad as me. She got tortured a lot about her hair because she did not have much. It was really, really short. Yet and still no one bothered her because they knew she had an older sister who would come to the school if she needed to.

One morning on the bus after picking Natasha up, she sat on the seat with me. There was someone else on the seat as well, but I do not know who it was. I sat in the middle and Natasha was on the outside near the aisle. I was having a bad morning because I woke up late and was rushing. I brushed my teeth as I usually do every morning, but I guess I still had a little morning breath. Natasha must have gotten a whiff of it on the bus.

I had Pre-Algebra second period. Ms. Bowman was the teacher. She was from England. I had to stay after class to finish up some class work and get some extra help because math did not come easy to me. I made A's and B's, but I had to work hard at it. We always had a short recess after second period. Mrs. Bowman's class was across from the bathroom on the seventh grade hall. I sat in the front of all my classes if I could.

Natasha, Libby, and Dayanna were coming out of the bathroom. Natasha said, "Yeah girl it was stanking on the bus." They laughed loud after that and continued down the hall to go outside. All I could think was, "Would it have hurt for them to offer me a piece of candy or gum? Why she just did not tell me my breath was a little funky?" I never had bad breath on a daily basis, but from that point on I always made sure I kept a piece of peppermint or gum.

By the eighth grade my siblings and I were living at home with our mom, which was next door to paw paw and granny. She started allowing me to attend sleep overs at my classmates' houses. It was probably more to her advantage than mine because the only times I spent the night at someone's house was when there was an event. In other words if I had a basketball game, softball game, track meet, or band concert it was more convenient for me to stay the night at someone's house to make sure I did not have to wait on what felt like an eternity for her to pick me up. It was embarrassing to be the last child picked up.

We lived about forty minutes from Ethel. We rode the bus for twelve years for a round trip of two hours per day. We lived in the country. It would have made perfectly good sense for us to go to school in Durant, MS. We could not though. Our house was right at the border line of Attala County and Holmes County, but because we lived on the Attala County side we had to attend an Attala County school.

Momma was never on time picking me up from any event after school. She was always late dropping me off at practice. Actually, it made sense for me to spend the night at someone's house. There were times when paw paw and granny picked me up, but that was just as embarrassing because of the car they drove. I was wise enough to ask girls who stayed out of trouble and come from respectable homes if I could spend the night.

Nickie and I were just about in everything together, but softball. Dayanna was on the softball team and basketball team with me. Ronda and Bella were on the softball team as well, but they lived closer to me than anyone else. Therefore, if we had a softball game Ardeshia and I caught a ride with them. Momma or paw paw and granny picked us up at a local store.

I did spend the night over Natasha and Libby house a few times. It was just because and come to think of it I did not ask. They invited me, but probably because I was in their group in class at school. They did not want to feel sorry for me or exclude me all of the time so they asked me out of pity. I felt like the third wheel or the odd man out so to speak. Dayanna spent the night as well. I always felt out of place especially when they discussed church.

We stopped going to church on a regular basis when I was nine. That was when my parents divorced. The only time we went was on Easter, Mother's Day, Father's Day, Christmas, or when someone invited us. That was when I got introduced to Baptist churches, which I grew to love. When I listened to those three talk about church, sometimes I understood and sometimes I did not.

Natasha's family went to a Pentecostal church. It was the same church we attended until the divorce. Libby and Dayanna attended a Baptist church. The one thing they got excited talking about was the choir. I always wanted to be in a church choir. They also got excited talking about Sunday school even though they were cracking jokes about what a member wore or how someone sounded, by the end of their conversation they always got serious and gave Jesus thanks. That always amazed me.

They said their prayers before going to bed. I just layed there or closed my eyes as they prayed. I did not really know how to say my prayers. I prayed and talked to Jesus day and night from my heart, but I wanted to learn the prayer they prayed. I took it upon myself to learn it and say it before I went to bed every night from that point on. The prayer was, "Now I lay me down to sleep. I pray the Lord my soul to keep. If I should die before I awake, I pray the Lord my soul to take. Amen." Once I learned that prayer, I felt a little more comfortable spending the night. My self-esteem was still very low. As they prayed I said the prayer to myself. I always told Jesus when he blessed me with a job and a car that I was going to church!

CHAPTER NINE

Ninth Grade

Bullying makes a person feel inadequate or belittles someone. It includes harassment, physical harm, demeaning speech, and efforts to ostracize another person. It is done with the intention of bringing another person down.

I finally began to find "LAKETTA" in the ninth grade. It was still about trying to "fit in," but INDIVIDUALITY was more important. I still had my eyes on Marquise. He finally began to notice me because I started dressing like a lady. We conversed from time to time especially in the morning in the auditorium. Due to my intelligence, it was not long before I realized no matter how strong my attraction was to him, it logically made no sense for me allow anything to go any further. It was hard too, but I did the right thing.

I started experimenting with make-up and high heels. One particular day I wore some blue jeans that fit kind of tight and a nice fitting red shirt. Donna was the first person to notice and say something nice. Her words were, "Ketta I've never seen you dressed like this. You really look nice and pretty. You need to dress like that more often." That was first thing in the morning once I got off the bus.

I asked to go to the bathroom during first period something I rarely did. I just had to see what Donna seen that day. I went to the bathroom on the seventh and eighth grade hall because it was bigger. The walls were all white with three full length mirrors. There were two white sinks with mirrors as well as four stalls. I stood in front of the mirror and just looked. One reason I did not like wearing jeans was because I was always told I had no butt or it was not big enough.

As I looked in the mirror like most girls did, I turned to the side and automatically looked at my butt. True enough it was not as big as the other girls, but I noticed other attributes on my body. My hips and thighs were developing. My breasts were perky and upright. I did not like my stomach area. I also had small love handles. Other than that I felt okay looking in the mirror. I wore the make-up to cover up the dark circles around my eyes. All of a sudden the boys who never paid any attention to me were noticing me. The girls could not stand me and began to "hate on me." I was not having sex nor degrading myself and some of the boys *still* liked me.

I caught the attention of Montell. He was a year older than me, but he was in my grade. We picked him up ninth grade year. He had a bright skin complexion with facial hair. He had dark, full eyebrows and mustache. He was just a little taller than me. He kept a low haircut. He was DaShay's nephew! He started walking me to the bus every evening. He walked me to some of my classes.

One day he wrote me a letter and I could definitely understand why he failed a grade. The letter basically asked me to be his girlfriend. I wrote one back and told him yes. I am not too sure how long we were a couple, but it did not end to well. His true colors began to show. He had a real bad temper and anger management problem. He was a "bad" boy. He had jealousy issues as well. He did not like to see another boy beside me or talking to me. I started trying to think of ways to break up with him without pissing him off.

One day I was walking to class. I was late because I stayed in my previous class to assist my teacher. She wrote me a pass to give my next period teacher to ensure I did not get a tardy. There was a little trail between the office building and the library as well as between the computer lab and the other end of the library building. I cut through the trail by the office to go to class. I was in no hurry of course because I had a pass. ☺ As I reached the end of the trail, I looked up and Montell was heading towards me coming from the other trail. I smiled as he walked toward me, but the closer he got I realized he was in a bad mood. I was still shy.

He stood in front of me and said, "Where the fuck you been? I waited to walk you to class and you never came!" Before I could say anything he slapped me as hard as he could. As usual I did not fight back or say anything, but I did not let him see me cry either. When I got home I went in the bathroom and cried my eyes out. I looked around to see who may have seen what just happened. Of course there was somebody late for class wandering school grounds. I do not know who it was, but he did not do or say anything at that moment. I later learned that he told others though.

The strange thing was after Montell hit me, he paused as if he could not believe what he did. I did not say one word. I turned and went to class. By the time I got out of fifth period the entire school knew. I felt ashamed and embarrassed. Once again I did not fight back and just allowed myself to be bullied and humiliated. Everyone was saying things like, "She got to be the stupidest person I know! I would've beat the shit out of him if he slapped me!" No one said anything to me directly, but I could hear the whispers once I entered a room, walked the hall, or went to the bathroom.

For a while Montell was walking around flaunting what he did. He was feeling like a "man." He was saying things like, "Hell yeah I hit that bitch! She knew not to hit me back cause I would have beat the fuck out of her!" As hard as it was I continued to wake up, go to school, and not entertain the gossip or rumors. Weeks passed and all of a sudden I received a letter as I was about to get on the bus. Somebody ran up and handed it to me. Once I got situated I opened it.

To my surprise it was from Montell. He apologized for what he did. He had the nerve to ask why I was not talking to him anymore. He wrote he was sorry in most of the letter repeatedly. The more I read the angrier I became, but I stopped and looked out the window. I took a deep breath and began to pray:

"Father I know you hear and always look out for me. Why can't I have a good life? I continue to try and live by your word, but I'm the one who keeps getting treated bad. Please take this hatred out of my heart toward Montell. Help me to forgive him. Amen."

Nickie and I became very close. We considered ourselves "best friends." She was tall and dark. She had a jerry curl and kept it cut short. She was skinny, but always thought she was fat! That was the one thing we had in common if nothing else. We became close during band season. I envied her so much. She had the "perfect family." Her mom Lydia and Bennie were married and still are. Not only did they have a good family, but they were great athletes as well. Coach Johnson adored them.

Her and Nick were extremely close. I never understood what people meant when they said, "twins have an internal connection," until I met them. The fact that they were fraternal twins made that concept even harder to grasp. Nickie got sick occasionally throughout the school year. She and I had the same class schedule every year with the exception of one or two classes. When she got sick it was as if Nick sensed it. He always came to her rescue.

We were in history class with Mr. McDaniel, the coolest teacher in the school. He got teacher of the year every year. Nickie told me she was not feeling to well. I did not think much of it. I told her that her "cycle" was probably about to come on. She caught hell when hers hit! Only this time when she went to the bathroom she was a gone a long time. I began to notice she was gone a long time. I walked up to Mr. McDaniel's desk and asked, "Can I go check on Nickie?" We had completed our assignment and were sitting in our desk doing whatever as long as we were quiet. He said, "Yeah and hurry back."

As I opened the door and was about to walk out, I noticed there was a crowd of people standing at the girl's bathroom door. Apparently a student had gone in to use the bathroom and found Nickie on the floor crying. Every teacher on the hall had come out of their room. They were either standing outside their door or at the bathroom door. As I began to walk down the hall I prayed nothing was seriously wrong. A girl walked passed and I asked, "What's going on?" She said, "Nickie in the bathroom crying on the floor. She say she can't move." I continued walking.

Then all of a sudden it was like when Jesus parted the Red Sea for the Egyptian slaves and Moses as they were running from Pharoah. Everyone moved to the side and Nick walked out of the bathroom with Nickie in his arms. I do not even know where he came from. She wrapped her arms around his neck. He carried her all the way down the hall outside down the ramp across the campus to the office. It was as if it all came to him so naturally. He was calm throughout the entire situation. After their mom came to get her, I went back to class. I was worried about Nickie all day. I called when I got home to check on her. Lydia said, "She doing okay. She sleeping. The doctor said the pain was coming from her ovaries." She eventually came back to school, but from that moment on she worried about being able to have kids. That was another thing we had in common, "WORRYING!"

We had a band recital one afternoon. Their house was walking distance from the school. We had to stay after school to get our uniforms and make sure our instruments worked properly and things to that nature. Mr. Doyle had been our instructor since the sixth grade. He was Caucasian and wore glasses. His hair was gray. He was balding in the top. He was tall and had a little pot belly. I never seen anyone take *pride* in teaching music the way he did.

Nickie always had guys wanting to date her. She always had a boyfriend. Ramon was her boyfriend at that time. He was supposedly my cousin. We rode the same bus and grew up together. He was very skinny, but the nicest guy anyone could meet. He played basketball too and was good at it. He was with us as we walked to their house.

Ethel was a very small town. Everybody knew everybody. There were two stores on the front street down the hill from the school. The kids always went to one store in particular to get their famous cheese sticks. They sold them five for one dollar. They resembled the ones now sold at Sonic Drive Inns across the nation. There was also a game room connected to the store. On game days or any other extracurricular activity day, we walked to the store and chilled out until it was time to perform or play.

As usual I was the odd girl out. I walked alone during those walks. We all walked together, but I walked way behind thinking and saying to myself, "God it has to get better than this ten years from now. I hope it does because I believe in the unseen, *faith*." Nickie and Ramon played around a lot. They had a goofy relationship, yet serious when needed be. She jumped on his back. He carried her all the way home sometimes. They kissed each other and things like that.

Nick was with Kiara. She was a senior at the time! She worked at the video store downtown, which was located next to the store with the arcade room. They were "in love." If I had to pick a couple from high school who I truly felt was in love it would have to be those two. I was devastated when they got together because I wanted Nick. Of course me being the person I was, I always hoped for the best. I always knew deep down inside she was going to hurt him.

As we walked sometimes they did not even miss me until we got to their house. That was when I became visible. Due to the fact that I had a great sense of humor or was a comedian at times, they never even noticed how down I was. They had a younger sister Cadence. She was the same age as Ardeshia. She walked beside me at times. I engaged in conversation with her so I did not feel alone.

The main thing that I envied the most when it came down to Nickie was the fact that her and Bennie had the best father-daughter relationship. I could only dream of having a relationship with my dad like that. They talked about everything. He was tall and dark with a jerry curl as well. He was overweight. He looked like he could have been an NFL center. He was big, but had the heart of an angel. Nickie talked to him about EVERYTHING especially boys. She valued his opinion. They all did, but Nickie was his heart. Even though Nickie and I were best friends I never told her the things I was going through. Even if I would have tried to, I would not have been able to. I was always listening to her talk about her problems. Or if I did try she eventually focused the conversation back on her and I forgot what I was trying to say anyway or put my thoughts to the side and focused on hers.

CHAPTER TEN

Tenth Grade

Verbal bullying is when someone uses words/language to destroy a person's self-image. It includes teasing, saying things to make a person feel they have no self-worth or not as important as others.

The juniors and seniors were mean, especially in the cafeteria. All they did was sit at their table, laugh and torment the seventh, eighth, and ninth graders as they came through the line. It was mostly Patricia, Orie, Rick, Mary, Donna, Cassandra, and many more.

The cafeteria was small of course because it was a 1-A school. There was a single door on the side with a ramp. The teachers and handicap students used that door. Sometimes regular education students used the door. There were double doors at the back of the building. Classes entered those doors and formed a line on the left to get their food. There was a kitchen area that was separated from the seating area by a wall with two single doors. One of the doors was were students entered to pick their tray up and proceed to tell the cafeteria workers what items they wanted to eat. The other door was where students exited to find a seat. The seventh grade sat on the far right. The twelfth grade sat on the far left. All the other grades were in the middle in order from right to left.

I had free breakfast and lunch, but because I feared what they may have said or done, I did not go in until lunchtime with my class. My tenth grade year during the first week of school I told myself things had to change. I was going to start eating breakfast. For three years once I got off the bus I found somewhere to "hide" basically because I just did not want to deal with the torment, torture, and bullying from my peers. I stood in a corner outside the cafeteria. Sometimes I stood by a teacher who was on duty, usually someone whose class I enjoyed or someone who took me under their wing. I found anything to talk about until the bell rung for first period. Other times I went in a bathroom no one used much.

Once I joined the high school band, I went in the band hall. The only students allowed in there was band members. It was all the way on the other side of campus and my first class was on the opposite side. Then on top of all of that once the bell rung, I did not walk under the walkway with other students. I walked around the side of the school to get to class.

I got off the bus and went toward the cafeteria. I took three deep breaths as I walked around the building toward the double doors. I prayed as I walked to the cafeteria:

"Jesus I know I get mad at you because I can't see what you are doing for me, but I still trust and have faith in you. I believe in you with everything in me. Please protect me as I walk through these doors. All I want is to eat breakfast in peace. I know I am not alone because you are always with me. If someone does bother me, give me the courage to be the bigger person, walk away, and pray for them. In your name, I pray. Amen."

I took one deep breath, lifted my head to the sky as if Jesus was looking right at me, and opened the door.

In the morning, we did not go as a class. As soon as we got off the bus it was our responsibility to go eat breakfast. Therefore, we sat where we wanted. It was still the same seating, (spoken, but unspoken). As I walked in everyone was quiet. There were not a lot of students in there. Those who were, lifted their head to see who was coming through the door. They looked at me and continued eating. I went through the line, which was not long and got my food. I sat by myself at the end of the table on the far right and ate in peace. I later began to notice that others who were ashamed, scared, or outcast also began to come in the cafeteria with me.

I was a LEADER and did not even know it. Actually, I did know. Jesus showed me a long time ago. I just did not want that responsibility at the time. Leaders set their own pace. Leaders understand what it is like standing alone because they are use to it. Leaders do their best work alone, and have to learn how to work well with others. Leaders are very spiritual and trust Jesus or some form of spiritual guidance to keep them grounded. Even though leaders are very successful and possess many characteristics, they too need a shoulder to cry on at times!

During football season, the band performed at every game during half time. We practiced all summer on formations and music in the hot sun. I did not know black people could get a "tan" until the first day of band camp. ☒ When it was hot, which was usually at the beginning of the season, we wore khaki pants and a black shirt with the school logo, mascot, and colors. I did not like wearing those pants because it made my butt look flat. Literally, it was as if I had no butt at all.

Ardeshia was my sister. She was two years younger than I. For as long as I can remember, I was always told that she was prettier than I. Leon made that perfectly clear in the fifth grade. The fact of the matter was that Ardeshia *was* gorgeous and I always envied her. She always spoke her mind when needed and did not let anyone run over her. She was quiet, but when she got offended, she had no problem saying so. I always wanted to have that characteristic about myself, but my soft-spoken heart did not allow me to. My motto was "kill them with kindness," "do unto others as you would have them to do to you," and allow Jesus to be my forefront.

Ardeshia and I played every sport together and were in band together. She played the trumpet. We were close, but not as close as I wanted to be. She always had a boyfriend or some boy fighting for her attention. She was with her boyfriend most of the time at school. I was her protector as I was for all of my siblings. I made sure no one bothered them. I most definitely made sure the boys treated her right. If they did not, they had to deal with me.

Blaine transferred to Ethel my tenth grade year. The girls went crazy because of how fine he was. He had the perfect body with washboard abs, rock hard butt, broad shoulders, strong arms, and firm chest muscles. He was slightly taller than average height of boys his age. He had a beautiful tan. He looked as if he could have been biracial, but he was Caucasian. He had dark brown hair. It was curly, but not too curly. He kept it cut low.

It was not long before he became the most popular kid in school. He was very athletic as well. He participated in every sport. His dad held the record at Ethel for the high jump event in track. Of course, out of all the girls who wanted to be his girlfriend, he chose an anorexic looking, blonde cheerleader who played softball. Her name was Ashley. There was only one thing wrong with Blaine. He had the nastiest attitude ever. He had too much pride and was very conceited. He was a spoiled brat who acted as if he had no home training. He appeared to be the perfect gentleman when around teachers and coaches, but when they were not around he was a jerk.

He was in my fifth period biology class. The teacher was Mrs. Janet Robertson. She was tall and petite. She had long brown hair, a gorgeous tan, and pretty blue eyes. She was tough as nails. She did not take any form of disrespect from no one, but she had the heart of an angel. She loved teaching biology and made it very clear to understand. She used many hands on activities, which I loved.

The class was in the lab preparing to dissect a pig for a week. My table group included Natasha, Ronda, Tyree, and myself. I was wearing glasses by then and no longer had a jerry curl. I had a perm and kept it cut short in a bob style. I had never really conversed with Blaine, but for some reason that day he decided to make hurtful jokes about my skin condition. I was a little more comfortable with wearing shorts by then.

Blaine started talking about me. He sat at the table directly behind me. He and Tyree started laughing. Neither of them liked to do class work. They always got in groups with "smart kids" or shall I say those of us who put forth the effort to do our work. They started cracking jokes on different kids in class. I had to have been the only one listening to what they were saying.

When they got to me, Blaine started saying things like, "She got spots on her leg like a Dalmatian. We should call her Spot." They were pointing at my legs and laughing. Blaine was laughing so hard that he turned red in the face. Tyree had a laugh that made a person laugh just by hearing him. When he laughed; his mouth flew wide open.

It had been a while since I got picked on about my skin condition. I was very hurt. I did not show it though. I continued doing my work and prayed they left me alone and moved on to the next joke. My table and Blaine's table got quiet. If their faces could have talked it would have said, "You got to be kidding me. Ya'll are mean, rude, and disrespectful." They were silently waiting to see what my reaction would be. I ignored them and continued working on our pig.

When the bell rung I slowly packed my things and went to history class with Mr. Montgomery. As I walked to class the tears began to develop in my eyes, but I gave myself the pep talk:

"Ketta you are better than them. Do not stoop to their
level. They will eat their words one day. Jesus please tell
them to leave me alone and not say harsh things."

We were going to be in the biology lab at least one more week and I did not want to be miserable.

By the end of History class I was feeling better. Mr. Montgomery had a great sense of humor. He always told jokes, but one had to be smart to understand the joke to laugh. He was an average height Caucasian. He was a much older teacher. He had to have been in his early forties. He wore big square glasses with a silver metal frame. What I liked about his class the most was the fact that he loved to get us involved in class discussions relating to chapters he introduced to us. He was into politics. I was never into politics, but I enjoyed watching him get excited when teaching political issues. I may not have understood what he was teaching, but his enthusiasm made me want to learn.

The next day in biology class I did not acknowledge Blaine or Tyree. It was if they were not even there. Mrs. Robertson had an assignment on the board and guess who needed help with their assignment, Tyree and Blaine! I politely told them no and continued to do my work. I made no eye contact or even turned my body toward them. Actually, Blaine put Tyree up to coming to me for help because he was too scared to say anything to me. He was use to his good looks and charm working for him all the time, but not with me.

As the class continued working on the assignment, I heard Blaine mumble something under his breath, "She ain't got to help me. That's why she got spots on her legs." I slowly turned around and looked in his direction to let him know that over all the noise in the lab, I heard him. He use to always bite his nails. When he realized I turned around, his entire face was red. I wanted to smile because I knew that he knew not to say those things anymore. I kept a straight face and maintained my ground. I was proud of myself. I immediately, took a deep breath, looked up toward the ceiling as if I could see the sky and said,

> "Thank you Jesus for giving me the wisdom to not fight fire with fire and allowing you to protect and guide me. Amen."

CHAPTER 11

Eleventh and Twelfth Grade

No More Pain

The eleventh and twelfth grade were good. I was no longer getting bullied nor was my self-esteem being affected as much as it was the previous years. As a matter of fact my self-esteem and confidence began to rise to a totally different, but good level. All of the bullies were gone. Either they graduated, dropped out, or the groups they use to hang out with were no longer at Ethel High School. Everyone had grown into that level of maturity. By that point it was time to decide what path to take when entering the "real world."

I was not the most popular girl in school, but my comedic personality and good grades earned me a good reputation. People began to want to be around me. Dayanna and I became best friends our senior year. We became really close because she got pregnant. I was the first person she told. She was dating Cortez who was my third cousin. He lived in my neighborhood in the country. They were the cutest couple. He was two years younger than her. They lost their virginity to each other. I always thought that was romantic and everyone did as well. They both were shy and quiet. He was shyer then she was. Everyone wanted what they had. Until they found out she was pregnant and he started cheating on her. I stood by her side throughout it all like a true friend supposed to only to end up hurt later on down the line.

My comedic personality gave me a little popularity. I was known as the class clown who did just about anything to make someone laugh. My teachers adored me. There was finally no more pain, at least not at school. My confidence level was slowly increasing. I was dressing more and more like a young lady. I wore high heels and everything. Ardeshia and I shopped together and brought matching outfits. My make-up was beginning to look flawless. I was a part of many organizations: Future Business Leaders of America (FBLA) secretary, BETA Club, Fellowship of Christian Students (FCS), Fellowship of Christian Athletes (FCA), Annual Staff, Band, Softball (hind catcher and first base), Basketball (point guard), Track (shot put), Student Council, and I did the morning announcements over the intercom (12th grade).

I got invited to the junior prom and ended up with a boyfriend to take me to my senior prom. His name was Tyree. The same boy who was my fourth grade boyfriend! He matured and reality set in. He wanted to do the right thing and graduate with his class. He took some form of test, which allowed him to do so. He was nervous that he was not going to pass the test, but he did. Believe it or not, I was not interested in him anymore. It was also hard for me to get past all the cruel things he said about me years prior.

He and Natasha were good friends. It was actually her who told me to give him a chance when he asked me to go to the prom. She fought hard to get me to give him a chance. He was a whore. He was always getting some girl to have sex with him or perform some sort of sexual activities. I did not want that type of guy. There were other attributes about him that eventually outweighed his whorish side. He had developed into a handsome young man. He had a gorgeous body. He had muscles that sent chills down my body every time he took his shirt off. His pectorals were hard and stood out. I always asked him to flex his arm muscles so I could feel them. He had washboard abs. His butt was solid. The muscles in his back were very defined.

On top of all of that, the brother dressed his butt off. He always had the flyiest outfits and current shoes. He still had a great sense of humor. He made anyone laugh. He did not like to see anyone feeling sad or depressed. He played football until he graduated. He was very respectful thanks to his grandma. She raised him. He truly had a big heart. It did not bother me about all the other things he did in the past because I knew he would one day eat his words! I decided that I might as well give him a chance, but I made him suffer for a few weeks before I gave him my answer. ⌧

He took me home for the first time after his prom rehearsal. I stayed after school to show him how to get to my house for prom. We sat in the car in front of my house. It was too cute because he took a deep breath, grabbed my hand, and said, "First of all I want to apologize for saying things to hurt your feelings. I was stupid. I really do want to be with you Laketta. I know you think I'm a player and no good, but I want you to be my girl. I'm done being with different girls." Inside I was excited and jumping for joy, but outside I had to be calm and serious.

While he was still holding my hands, I told him to look me in the eyes. I said, "You know I'm not going to tolerate any disrespect. I would never ask you to do something you were not ready to do. I want you to be sure this is what you really want. I'm still a virgin and plan on keeping it that way for a long time. Can you handle all of that?" He never took his eyes off of me. He responded, "Laketta I'm ready." We officially became a couple on May 12, 1998. We ended up being in a serious relationship for two years. I was sad when he graduated because I finally had a nice, handsome guy who treated me with respect and no one was going to see it. I wanted the school to see how happy I was. He did not pressure me into sex, which was great.

I ran for homecoming queen my senior year. It was just something to do. My self-esteem was getting better as well as my confidence. I still did not think I was pretty and definitely not going to win homecoming queen. I played it smart and knew that the biggest classes were the seventh and eighth graders. Every chance I got I was on their hall asking them to vote for me. The announcements were read over the intercom every morning by a senior. On that day they were done by an office worker and she said, "The nominees for the 1999 homecoming court are Rachel and Laketta Lowery." Of course she announced them for every grade, but everyone only listened to the senior names. I was in Mr. Montgomery's class when I heard my name. I could not believe it. It happened so fast. Everyone was saying congratulations. I was sitting in my desk shocked, not moving and barely saying thank you.

Rachel was Caucasian and a very good friend of mine. She was short, about my height. She had long blonde hair with brown streaks. She was a thick girl. She felt like an outcast as well at times because she felt she was not as pretty or smart as Donna, Ronda, or Chloe. She confided in me from time to time about things she was going through. I will never forget her for one reason.

Birthdays have always been important to me. I never ask for anything, but a birthday card. No one ever made a big deal about my birthday, especially my family. I can count on one hand how many birthday parties I had growing up. I never asked for much. It just meant the world to me to hear a person say, "Happy Birthday Ketta," on the actual day of my birthday. It meant the world to me to receive a card and nothing more. She remembered my birthday in the eleventh grade and brought me a card. She gave it to me in our homeroom, which was Mrs. Gardner that morning. We became very close friends after that.

My little brother, Shaun was my escort homecoming. He was fourteen at the time and was more nervous than I was. I was not nervous at all. He had on a white tuxedo. I had on a long silk blue dress. It did not have any straps and fell off of my shoulders. It also had a split on the right side that stopped at my knee. Mom had a lady she knew to make the dress. My hair had waterfalls.

After we were all on the field and everyone was announced as we walked down the football field, Mrs. Robertson came on the microphone. She had a loud mouth and a heart of gold. She said, "Your 1999 homecoming queen is......Laketta Lowery." I looked over at Rachel and before I could say anything, she said, "Congratulations." It was extremely loud outside. Therefore, I read her lips. I said, "Thank You." My mom recorded the entire event. Over all the noise, the only person I heard and focused on was my mom's. She was standing at the fence directly in front of where Shaun and I were standing yelling, "That's my baby. That's my baby." For that reason and that reason only, that night meant the world to me. When the crown was placed on my head and I received the flowers to hold in my arms, I felt like a beautiful princess. Barriers were broken that night as well because I was the first African-American to win homecoming queen in ten years!!! *I was no longer the ugly duckling. I had developed into the beautiful swan.*

CHAPTER 12

You Reap What You Sow

Growing up I always told myself that I was going to be the first girl in the NBA. I was going to be the first on to dunk! That's right me, 5'1" and wanting to dunk. Don't criticize me, is that now what kids do *DREAM* and *BELIEVE!*

Sadly, that dream never came true. The older I got during high school I began to wonder many things in terms of athletes. How was it that God blessed the best athletes with the greatest gift and everybody realized that except the athlete? Why did the athletes who were not as talented as those who were have more heart? How could the best athletes make bad grades in class or fail a grade? Why do the best athletes have the worst attitudes? How was it that the best athletes received scholarships to pay for college and they only went for a few years and quit or turned down the chance others only dreamt of? A person such as myself would have given anything to set foot on a college gymnasium on a basketball scholarship. Then graduate college and have the greatest opportunity in the world to play for a WNBA team. Deep down inside I still hold on to that dream. Now I envision myself walking on a college or WNBA court as a coach!

There were many athletes who went to school with me who everyone felt should have been very successful in the world of sports: Craig, Mia, Jamal, Mia, Blaine, DaShay, and Marquise. There were several other athletes, but these were unstoppable. Why? What happened? Life happened! Were they bullied by teammates and felt God's wrath of "you reap what you sow?"

DaShay tore a ligament in her knew during a basketball game her senior year. I remember seeing the desperation in Coach Johnson's face the following day of school. I know what it is like to lose a key player. Two of my starting basketball players hurt their knee right before playoffs started. Coach Johnson did what any other coach would have done. After her surgery, he nursed her back to health. He bought a stationary bike from his house and put it in the gym. It was on the sideline. Once DaShay was released from the doctor and took off her crutches and knee brace, she rode that bike. He made sure she got on it every day during practice.

She eventually got to play again, but something was different. Her skills and ability was okay, but I began to notice a change in her personality. She was still quiet, but much nicer. As if the surgery was not enough, she got pregnant! Coach Johnson never really said anything, but I knew he was disappointed. What coach wouldn't be? She was a leading scorer and by far the best athlete on the team. I am sure he was asking himself, "What am I going to do now Lord?" She did not play ball after high school.

Once she graduated I did not see her again until I was twenty or twenty-one. Coach Johnson had some type of event at Greenlee for a week one summer. Aunt Sandy had her kids in it. Friday of that week Coach Johnson hosted a basketball game for the girls. It was adult women versus young girls and teenage girls. It was not a lot of people there. Sandy asked me to play at the last minute because they did not have enough adults. I was young and they needed some energy. To my surprise, DaShay, was there. By then she had two kids. They were in the events for the week as well. Coach Johnson must have invited her to play.

Ever since I graduated high school, I took it upon myself to improve in basketball, to not be intimidated by anyone and to play from my heart. I was good and I knew it. I could not wait to play and show Coach Johnson how good I was, how running was not a problem for me anymore because I started jogging every morning at seven in my neighborhood. I still jog this very day. The adult team consisted of Sandy, DaShay, me, and about three more adults. The youth team had about ten players. They rotated in and out. I played the entire game. My position was still the point guard.

Coach Johnson threw the ball up in the air and DaShay tipped it. I ended up with the ball. I showed up and showed out! I came to play ball. I was making those no look passes, playing defense, running the floor, and making baskets. The best part of the entire game was when I heard DaShay say, "Damn Ketta! Why you didn't play like this in school? You good girl." I did not say much to her as we walked on the court. A part of me wanted to take that ball from Coach Johnson and throw it in her face. I have never been one to talk smack as I play unless I was being goofy. I take the game very serious. I am very competitive. I love to compete and win. When I heard her say that, I had just hit her with a no look pass as she stood on the block. I penetrated down the lane and dished it off to her. She made that comment as we got back on defense.

I could not believe it. I got a compliment from DASHAY. I was on top of the world for the rest of the day. We won of course, but as I was on my way home I could not help but think in response, "If you would not have been so mean or took the time to get to know me or took into consideration what I was dealing with, I would have played the way I did today." I looked to the sky and said, "Thank you Jesus!"

Blaine graduated high school successfully. As athletic as he was and out of all the colleges he had trying to recruit him, he chose to go to the Navy. He and Ashley continued their relationship after graduation, but I am not sure how long. I worked in Subway in Kosciusko for four years. One of my classmates Aubrey came in one day, and we were just catching up and letting each other know what was going on in our lives. She ended up telling me how Blaine got kicked out of the Navy and was living at home with his parents. I was twenty-one at the time. I could not believe it.

True enough I could not stand him and still carried a grudge against him for how he treated me, but I would not wish anything like that on anyone. Surprisingly, a few weeks later Blaine came to Subway to eat. I noticed him once he got to the door. It had not dawned on him who I was yet because a sista looked very different from the last time he seen me. ☒ He got stopped at the door by someone he knew I guess. They talked for a minute. As they talked I remember thinking, "Damn he still looks the same. Fine as I don't know what!" I quickly shook that thought and snapped back to reality.

He glanced over during his conversation and finally realized who I was. He turned red in the face. As soon as the man he was talking to walked out, I went to the back of the store to act as if I was getting something. I watched the monitors above the prep table, which were there to let the employees know when customers were in the store. He stood at the door leaning over one of the tables in the lobby. He could not believe it was me. His face was still red with embarrassment. He knew I had been told what happened to him. The next thing I knew, he turned and hurried out the door!

Frida had at least two kids by Thomas, one of the biggest whores who attended school with us. They were living with his mom a year after graduation. They eventually got their own place. He constantly cheated on her in high school. The only reason he was even with her was because of sex. He tried to pull those player cards on me, but I never fell for them. Besides he was so not my type anyway. I preferred clean cut men with gorgeous muscular bodies. Hygiene was a must. That was one thing he had a problem with especially his mouth. He did not brush his teeth and had plaque buildup for days on them. I never understood how anyone kissed him.

Frida stood by his side though. He continued to cheat because the last time I seen him, he tried to get with me. He kept saying, "Damn you fine. Damn. I'm gonna give you my number. Call me please. What she don't know won't hurt her. I will give you anything you want." It would have been the sweetest revenge from what she did to me for all those years, but I have a heart. If I was married I would want the woman to have the same respect for me. I was on cloud nine after that.

Keiona dropped out of school. She married a man named T. J. from another city. They moved into an apartment in Philadelphia, MS. They lived their shortly. Then moved to his hometown, which was closer to where we were from. They had kids eventually, but the marriage took a turn for the worse. She divorced him and moved in a house next to her mom.

Surprisingly, throughout the years we became close. We always cracked jokes on each other and laughed together. She always said, "Ketta you silly and crazy. You ain't got no sense!" We hung out from time to time. Once I moved to attend college in Jackson, MS I did not see her anymore. She came to my college graduation party and that was the last time I seen her. Ardeshia called me a year later and told me Keiona died in a car accident. Her body was thrown from the car. She was going to fast in a curve and lost control. The accident occurred around three o'clock in the morning. I did not attend the funeral.

Leon did a complete 360. Once we got to Ethel, I did not see him much. He was an okay athlete. He played on the football team until we graduated. He let his hair grow long and kept it braided. Everyone thought that between he and Kendrick, Leon was going to be the one who drop out of school and choose the wrong path in life. Boy was we wrong and totally surprised. Leon graduated with us. Kendrick decided two months before graduation that he was going to drop out. I could not believe it. I saw him a few years after graduating high school while I was working at Subway.

He came in with some girl to get something to eat. He appeared to still be quiet and shy, but he did not look the way he used to. He looked rough as if he was living his life to fast. He was not dressed clean like he usually did. His lips were black, which only meant one thing, he was a smoker. After paying for his food, he gave me that Kool-Aid smile and spoke. They left after that. I later learned the girl he was dating was from West, my hometown. He also smoked marijuana. The last time I saw him was at my granny's church. His dad was the pastor. It was Easter Sunday. Kendrick and his girl came. They sat in the very back. I kept sneaking glances at him. He had his head down most of the time. After church I thought, "I can't believe how he turned out. Life has a strange way of dealing one a bad hand, but what's important is how the hand is played."

Leon went to welding school. He graduated successfully. He lives in Mississippi. He married Larissa who also graduated from Ethel a year after our class. They have a son. They have only been married for a few years. Ardeshia and I were shocked to see those two together.

Leon had the biggest crush on Ardeshia. She worked with me at Subway as well. He came up there one time to see her. I was off that day, but she could not wait to tell me when she got home. She said, "Girl he got a Mustang, the new one. It's green and he fine! He still got his hair braided. It's longer than it was in school. He got rims on the car too." From time to time on my way to work I passed him in his car. I never saw him face to face anymore after school. I did not want to see him. I was afraid of what I might to do to him.

I got very sick when I was twenty. I was put on bed rest for a few weeks. Some kind of way Montell found out. He came to my mom's house almost every day to check on me. He talked with momma and everything as I was laying on the couch. I could not believe it. He still looked the same at that moment. I do not remember everything they said, but I do remember him asking, "Ms. Veronica what happened?" Momma said, "I don't know. Ketta do so much. She don't talk to no one or let anyone know what's going on with her. She keep everything bottled up inside." The doctor wants her to rest a few days." He said, "Let me know if you need anything. I'm gonna keep coming to see her." He did just that. He drove his grandmother's car or had someone bring him to my house.

As I began to feel better he and I engaged in conversation about a lot of things. We never talked about what he did to me in high school. He did tell me over and over again how he wanted me to be his woman! He wanted to take care of me. I thought about it for a second because I never had anyone to take care of me, especially in a relationship, but I quickly shook that thought. Montell sold drugs and I definitely did not want a man like that by my side.

As we was sitting at the kitchen table talking, he was actually playing with some salt. He poured it from the salt shaker mom had on the table. Then he took a piece of paper and separated it as if it was cocaine. When he realized what he was doing he said, "My bad. See I do this shit so much that it comes naturally to me." I thought to myself, "Are you freaking serious? I got to get him out of my mom house."

We walked outside to his car. I hugged him and said, "I don't know how you knew I was sick, but thank you for checking on me." He said, "No problem. I'm really feeling you Ketta. I will do anything for you. All you have to do is ask." He got in the car and drove off. He called from time to time and even stopped by Subway, but I ignored him and hid in the back of the store until he left.

Two years later I ran into him again. This time it was at a chicken plant in Carthage, MS called Tyson. I worked there one month during the summer and called it quits. I felt like a slave for real. I take my hat off to anyone whose occupation is in a chicken plant. My cousin Janiya and I drove to work together. We were on break one day when she said, "Oooohh girl there go Montell." We were sitting outside and as soon as she said that he started walking towards us.

My initial instincts were to get up and run to a different direction, but that would have been rude. Once he made it to where we were he said, "What's up Janiya. You still look the same girl." She was being goofy as usual and sniggling looking toward me. She finally responded, "Hey Montell." Then he looked at me. I was looking everywhere but at him. I knew he was not going to take *NO* for an answer. At that moment I knew I was going to be ducking and dodging him when I came to work.

He said, "What's up Ketta. You can't speak?" I felt my blood begin to boil. He could be so negative and rude at times because he spoke his mind. When people speak their minds they can come off as being rude or disrespectful because they do not think before they speak. It is not *what* you say, but *how* you say it! I made eye contact finally and said, "I only speak when spoken to. Besides when you walked up you said what's up to Janiya." Then I finally said, "Hey Montell." Break was up, "Thank God," I thought. I quickly got up. Janiya did too. We joined in with our co-workers and went back inside.

Janiya cracked jokes on me the remainder of the day. I was right of course because Montell followed me all over that plant for the rest of the week. He looked horrible too. His beard and mustache was all over the place. He had an afro that was all over his head. It was not neat at all. He gave me his phone number at some point, but I never called. He followed me so much that he was "blocking" any other man who wanted to holla at me. ☺ I definitely did not like that!

He must have stood outside one Friday and waited until we got off because as soon as we set foot in the parking lot, he started walking with us. Janiya spoke and made a call on her cell phone. Then she walked on to the car. Montell and I walked slowly. He asked, "Why haven't I heard from you? Why you don't call me?" Calmly I responded, "I'm gonna be honest with you. The last thing I need right now is a relationship. I have too much going on. I'm getting ready to go to college. I look after my sisters and brother. I work full-time. I'm just not interested in you like that Montell."

We both paused and stood still. My heart was beating so hard I thought it was going to come through my chest. I knew he still had an anger management problem. I did not know if he was going to put his hands on me again like in high school. I do not know if my heart was beating fast because I thought he was going to hit me or because I feared I would try and kill him if he did! He finally said, "That's all you had to say. You could have told me that last week." He turned and walked off. I exhaled, looked to the sky and said, "You always keep your angels around me. Thank you Jesus."

It is amazing how life works out. The things that one does in early childhood and teenage years dictate the way their lives will turn out. The ones who were considered "fine," ten years later will not look that way. If you are a teenager reading this book, be careful how you treat people. The one boy/girl who you think is ugly will be a "dime" so to speak ten years later. They could have the biggest crush on you and want to be your husband/wife, but emotional damage will be too much for them to get past. The nerd you tortured may end up being the one who repairs your cell phone or laptop ten years from now. The athlete who played on your team, but rode the bench most of the season just may work hard and become a professional athlete who your kid wants to go see play. The gay kid you tormented daily could very well end up being a defense attorney on which *your* kid is on trial.

If you are an adult reading this book and were bad and disobedient growing up. Then nine times out of ten your children will be ten times worse than you were. Truthfully, there will be nothing you can do about it. If you bullied someone growing up, there is a big possibility that your child will end up getting bullied as well. There will be nothing you can do about it. One may think that is not true, but think about it. Would your child really tell you they were getting bullied? I think not because of fearing you would probably beat the hell out of them for letting someone bully them! Some call it karma, some call it life, some call it growing up and kids being kids, but one day those kids will be adults just as you once were and when their life take a turn for the worst, they will wonder why. The answer is everywhere, just look at society and the problems they face. I look at in a spiritual sense of course. It all comes back to you. You get out what you put in. *Therefore, you reap what you sow!*

PART II: TEACHING EXPERIENCES

CHAPTER 13

My Calling

The three years that I taught was a blessing. Just about every day at work, I looked around as if I was dreaming. All of my hard work paid off. I kept the faith and Jesus remembered! I sat in my office crying tears of joy and constantly saying, "Thank you Jesus!" I taught Physical Education, Health, and was the head coach for the girls' basketball team at Pearl Junior High School. I was good at it too especially the teaching. One of my professors at Jackson State University said, "In order to be a great coach you have to be the best teacher." I knew I was going to be a good teacher. I wanted to inspire and reach children in ways one never thought was possible. During that summer prior to my first teaching year when I prayed I always said, "Jesus if I do nothing else in my career please allow me to reach just one child."

I taught at a junior high school where the grades were sixth, seventh, and eighth. I was nervous about coaching because I had never done it before. I did not have an assistant either. When I received the call letting me know I was hired, Mr. Sharpe informed me that the PE position came along with a coaching position. He asked, "Would you be willing to coach a seventh and eighth grade team as well as teach PE?" My response was, "Yes sir!"

I ended up reaching more than I could have ever imagined. My door was always open for students. They knew they could come to me for anything and that I would be there for them the best way I could. I had students coming to talk to me about everything. I could be eating in the cafeteria and they came talk to me as I ate. Whether I was on duty, in between classes, during class, or getting ready to go home, if they needed me they found me! I LISTENED, gave advice, and PRAYED with my students. They came to me with all kind of issues: family, drugs, relationships, sex, peer pressure, bullying, self-esteem, pregnancy, suicide, and teachers!!! Most of the students came to me for bullying issues, *go figure!*

CHAPTER 14

Racardo

Boys use bullying as a way of expressing their emotions toward the opposite sex.

The first bullying situation was centered around the sixth grade. Coach Harrington who also taught Health, came to my office one day. He and I actually graduated from Jackson State University the same year. He was African-American and FINE!!! He had a gorgeous body. It was very defined. His lips were big and juicy. His skin complexion was smooth and dark like a Hershey's chocolate bar. He was very quiet and shy or so most people thought. If I were allowed to choose any man to be my husband, it would have definitely been him. Of course my feelings were hurt when I later learned he had gotten married.

He had a young lady, Kennedy, who was being bullied by a boy. His name was Racardo. They were both African-American. I later learned that he was in one of my classes. Kennedy was a very pretty, shy girl. Her complexion was light brown. That was my first time seeing her. Coach Harrington informed me that Kennedy had been getting bullied by Racardo for quite a while. Surprisingly, she emailed her teachers whose classes Racardo took with her to inform them about the bullying. Coach Harrington was the only one who took it serious. As a matter of fact he was probably the only one who actually read the email. It was a cry for help and we were the only two who responded!

Coach Harrington had Kennedy in his third period class, which was my planning period. He pulled Kennedy in the hall, but before doing so he came to my office and asked me to come with him for a minute. He asked her to tell me what she told him. She had big brown eyes with a big forehead. She wore her hair in a ponytail. As she looked up at me her eyes began to tear up. She proceeded to tell me what was going on.

When she went to her locker Racardo was always there trying to keep her from getting her books out. He slammed it in her face. Then stood there and looked at her. She was late for her classes because of that. Sometimes on her way to class he walked behind her and threw things at her. I began to analyze everything Kenya told me. "Why was he bullying her?" I thought. I immediately thought it was because he had a crush on her. Boys are stupid at that age. They are not in touch with their emotions and if they are, they have no clue how to express them. Then I thought maybe he just did not like her and wanted to be mean to her the way Leon was to me.

Racardo was in my second period class. After checking roll, monitoring the students as they performed their stretching exercises, and giving instruction for the day, I pulled Racardo to the side. He was tall and a little overweight. His skin complexion was medium brown. He had dimples that were clear to see when he smiled. He had sandy brown hair, which he kept cut low. He was quiet and shy as well. He was very respectful and did not give me any trouble in class. He was very well-mannered, which also led me to believe that he came from a good home. He was very active and participated in PE daily.

As he walked towards me he dropped his head. I was an authoritative teacher. I expected the best from *ALL* of my students. As long as they followed the rules and showed respect I was okay. I was not the "sit down" kind of teacher. I interacted with the children. I participated in the activities at least two or three days a week. I played, motivated, and refereed.

He knew he was in trouble, but he did know not what for. We stood on the side next to the bleachers. I said, "Raise your head and look me in the eyes." Once he lifted his head I asked, "Do you know Kennedy?" He responded, "Yes ma'am." His eyebrows rose and his forehead crinkled up as if he knew he was busted. I informed him that Kennedy had come to me and told me he was bullying her. I asked, "Do you have crush on her?" He said, "No Ma'am." I continued, "Why are you treating her that way?" He looked at me and said, "I don't know." I told him to sit down in the bleachers. I sat down beside him. I talked to him about my childhood experiences.

As he sat there, his posture was slouched. His hands and arms were on his legs. His head was slightly down. When I told him how I was bullied and the affects it had on my life, he lifted his head in astonishment. He could not believe it. As I continued telling him what happened, he realized he had made a big mistake. After our conversation I told him he had two options for punishment: 1) I could write him up and turn it in or 2) I could find my own way to punish him. He chose option two of course. For the rest of the week I had him doing chores in the gym. He swept the bleachers, cleaned the doorways, and picked up clothes the kids left in the bleachers. I had a "lost and found" box that I put items that the kids accidently left behind in.

The following week I went to Coach Harrington's room during third period to speak with Kennedy. I wanted to see if things had gotten better as far as Racardo was concerned. She looked at me again with tears in her eyes and softly said, "Coach he still bothering me. I don't know what else to do."

Coach Harrington and I decided to team up and strategize to solve the problem. We knew Racardo was going to be an athlete. I told Coach Harrington I was going to call his parents first. Then we could go from there if his parents could not get through to him.

Immediately after speaking with Coach Harrington, I went to my office to call his mom. I was shocked as I talked to her. She was a nurse. I cannot remember what his dad's occupation was, but it was a good one. He came from a stable home just as I suspected. Of course, she said he was a good kid. What parent does not!!! She told me he was into sports and how she and his dad both played sports growing up. After she got all off the subject of what I called for, I quickly reminded her why I called. She assured me she would talk to him when he got home. I told her I was going to do all I could to get through to him. She told me that was okay and to let her know if I needed anything else.

The next day I pulled Racardo to the side and said, "I spoke to your mother. We both are very disappointed in you. One day you are going to have kids and the same way you treated Kennedy, someone is going to treat your kids. It's going to be ten times worse and there is not going to be anything you can do about it!" I could tell I was getting through to him. I continued, "Your mother gave me the okay to punish you until you understood that bullying was not nice. You are going to run around the gym for me the remainder of the week while the rest of your classmates have fun and enjoy PE. Once again you have two options: 1) take the write up and have it on your file or 2) take my punishment with no write up." He dropped his head and said, "I will do what you want me to coach." I allowed him three water breaks as he ran. On the last day of running I could tell he learned his lesson.

I called him in my office when he finished to have one last talk with him. I explained, "I know you are a good kid, which is why I can't understand the bullying. I asked him one last time, "Do you have a crush on Kennedy?" Before he answered I said, "There is another approach you can and should take, write her a letter or JUST BE NICE. If I did not believe or have faith in you to do the right thing, I wouldn't have punished you the way I did." He looked at me and said, "I know coach and I won't let you down again. I'm sorry." I stood up, walked over to him and made him get up. I hugged him and said, "Don't be sorry, just fix it!" I love you and I'm always praying for you."

CHAPTER 15

Bay Bay

It is very important to understand that sometimes the child who is bullied can turn into a bully. It ends up being a repeated cycle.

My second year teaching there was a seventh grade African American student who came to my office one afternoon. Her name was Santianna, but those who knew her called her "Bay Bay". She was actually on my basketball team. She was short and chubby, but that girl could play some basketball. She had short hair and looked mean sometimes. She had an attitude as well, but not with me. Jesus blessed me with a gift and the patience to teach and reach children with those characteristics. She was also quiet and kept to herself at least her sixth and seventh grade year. ☺

On one particular day, Bay Bay came in my office and sat down. She said, "Coach I got a friend who is getting bullied. She asked me what to do about it and I don't know what to tell her." At first, I was thinking Bay Bay was getting bullied, but then I thought to myself, "Naw, she to strong and dominant for that." I asked, "Where and when do most of the bullying taking place?" She said, "On the bus and on the weekends when she outside playing in her neighborhood." I asked, "Was it a girl or boy doing the bullying and how old were they?" She replied, "A girl and she is fourteen." I asked, "Do I know the bully?" She looked at me and without hesitation said, "Yes. Her name is Jeanette." I did not remember her at first, but when Bay Bay told me she took PE and had Coach Harrington, I knew exactly who she was. She was big and tall. She was African-American as well with a medium brown skin complexion. She had a big stomach. She really did look like a bully. Sometimes she wore glasses that slid down her face. They sat on the edge of her nose.

As I continued to listen to Bay Bay, I realized that it *WAS* her and not a "friend." I looked her in the eyes and said, 'Bay Bay are you the one getting bullied?" She raised her head slowly. The tears began to roll down her face. She started crying extremely hard. I was mad inside because I looked at the basketball team as if they were my own children. I wanted nothing more than to find Jeanette and beat the crap out of her.

I stood up and walked slowly to the other side of my desk where she was sitting. She was very tough and did not like people to see her cry. She had this protective shield where she did not let anyone get close to her. I told her to stand up. I gave her a big hug. As I hugged her, she let out a big sigh of relief and she squeezed me as if she had not hugged anyone in years. I asked, "Why didn't you tell me sooner?" Still crying, she said, "I don't know coach. I just don't know coach." I softly told her to straighten her face up and sit down so that we could figure out how to resolve the problem. I sat back on my side of the desk.

I could see the relief on her face already. It was as if the sun was peeking through the blinds in a house early on a Sunday morning. I asked, "Do you want me to talk to Jeanette?" I knew that if I talked to her she may bully Bay Bay even worse. I asked, "Do you want me to call your parents and inform them of what's going on?" She quickly said, "No coach don't do that! They hardly at home anyway because they work so much." I looked at her and calmingly said, "Bay Bay what do you want me to do?" She responded, "Talk to Jeanette coach. Just please talk to her." I asked, "Would you feel okay if I had Jeanette and you in my office at the same time?" She hesitated at first as she pondered that question. I interrupted her thought and continued, "You need to tell Jeanette what you feel. She may not know she is bullying or hurting your feelings. Nine times out of ten she doing it because of peer pressure. I will be right here with you." She responded, "Okay." I wrote her a pass to go to third period.

I took my fourth period, which were sixth graders, to lunch every day. The seventh grade girls' basketball team met me in the cafeteria to eat as well. I was responsible for two groups during lunch! I stopped by the counselor's office on our way back to the gym to find out where Jeanette was fifth period. After eating lunch, the sixth graders used the bathroom and sat in the bleachers until the bell rang to exchange classes. The basketball girls got dressed and got on the floor to do their stretches. It was routine. I pulled the team captains to the side, which were Macy, Jolie, and Bay Bay. I told Macy and Jolie what to direct their teammates to do until I got back. I told Bay Bay went to my office.

I went to get Jeanette. I am not sure what teacher she had, but I knocked on the door and asked to see Jeanette for a moment. That teacher was glad for me to get her. She responded, "Of course you can. Keep her as long as you want!" As we walked to the gym it was silent. I was in front and Jeanette was walking slowly behind me.

I opened the door to my office. Bay Bay was sitting in my chair behind the desk. Jeanette dropped her head as soon as she seen Bay Bay. I looked at Bay Bay and I could see the intimidation on her face. I told Jeanette to sit in the chair on the other side of my desk. I stood because I wanted Bay Bay to be comfortable. I did not want to allow them to sit beside each other in case a fight broke out.

I looked at Jeanette and asked, "Do you know why you are in here?" She replied, "No ma'am." I asked, "Do you have a problem with Bay Bay? She replied, "No ma'am." My next question was, "If you have no problems with her, then why do you bully her?" There was complete silence in my office for at least five minutes. Bay Bay had a little confidence and that was probably because I was in there with her. The look on her face lead me to believe she was ready to jump across my desk at any moment.

Jeanette on the other hand was scared and nervous. She had no clue what I was going to do. I honestly think she was very shocked that Bay Bay told on her. It was just amazing because she had no clue that the things she did or said to Bay Bay was bullying. She did not know she was torturing her. I broke the ice and told my personal stories about bullying. The looks I got from students as they listened to what happened to me was priceless. I appeared strong and was not the kind of person to take anything from anyone and they could not believe someone like me was BULLIED.

After I finished telling Jeanette about my experiences, I asked, "How bad do you want to play basketball. Without hesitation she said, "Coach I want to play bad. I play every day when I get home. I was mad because I did not make the team." I continued, "The main reason I did not put you on my team was because I felt you would cause a lot of drama and problems with the other girls. It appears that I was right because you in my office." I looked at Bay Bay and asked, "Do you love playing basketball? How much do love playing basketball?" She replied, "Coach you know I love playing basketball. I play every day." I continued, "Look at it this way, one day you two just might end up playing on the high school team together. Let's say you two are in a game together or practice for that matter and you are wide open for a shot. Do you think Bay Bay will pass you the ball? Better yet do you think ya'll will have good chemistry or bad chemistry during practice or a game?"

Girls are very emotional and everything affects the way they play. I continued, "She may never forgive you for bullying her and that alone could cause you all to have a bad season. You are the oldest and it is apparent that you are a leader because you always have a group of girls following you and mimicking what you do. It is time for you to be accountable for your actions. Someone is always watching you, wanting to be just like you, and be cool just like you. But if you are not setting a good example, what will the ones behind you have to go by? If you bully Bay Bay, she may end up bullying someone the same way you did her if not worse. When you all get to the high school and play together, I want to hear good things. I want to come watch ya'll play good together and have a good season. Do you understand everything I am saying?"

By that time she was slouched in her chair and looking at the wall. She knew I was disappointed in her. She slowly looked at me and replied, "Yes ma'am." I said, "I want you to apologize to Bay Bay, but only if you are going to mean it." She looked over at Bay Bay and said, "I'm sorry. I did not know that I was being mean to you or hurting your feelings. Please forgive me." Bay Bay responded, "Whatever. I forgive you." I asked them to stand up as I led them in prayer:

> "Dear Heavenly Father thank you for allowing me to guide these young ladies in the right direction. Please watch over them and take the hate out of their hearts towards each other. Most importantly once they leave my office and go around their peers give them the strength and courage to stand up for what's right. They know who *YOU* are Father and that you are the only one who can ease their pains and take away their problems. Hear their prayers Father and touch their hearts. In your name I do pray, Amen."

A week went by and I began to worry because I had not heard anything about the situation. I pulled Bay Bay to the side during practice and asked her to stop by my office after she got dressed. She came in and was in a good mood. I couldn't help but ask, "How are things going between you and Jeanette?" She said, "Everything okay coach. She still acting a little mean, but not towards me." She turned to walk out the door, but not before turning around and saying, "Thank you coach for always being there for me." I responded, "No problem that is what I am here for. Let me know if you need anything else."

CHAPTER 16

Heather

There are a lot of special education children who get bullied every day. Some teachers and especially parents do not care to recognize it."

Schools are now implementing "inclusion programs." Inclusion allows special education children to attend classes with regular education children. I was always excited to teach special education children. They challenged me to see if I had what it took to create lessons plans and activities that incorporated their mental and physical abilities.

My last year teaching was when I met Heather. She was very shy and quiet. She was in the sixth grade and Caucasian. She was taller than me of course and wore glasses. She came in my office at least three times a week to borrow a pair of PE shorts. She kind of slurred her words when she talked as well as talked with her tongue. She came to me one day and I assumed she needed a pair of shorts as usual. I was sitting at my desk doing some paper work. I looked up and said, "The box is behind the door sweetie. Look in there and get you a pair." As she walked toward the front of my desk, she said very softly, "Coach Lowery can I talk to you for a second?" I stopped what I was doing and gave her my undivided attention. I said, "You sure can. Have a seat and talk to me." Her glasses were very thick and she had shoulder length brownish hair. She was scary and intimidated as well.

As she sat down she made no eye contact and had her head down. She began to talk, "Coach I'm sad and I don't want to go home today. I just don't like going home anymore." The first thing that came to my mind was that someone was molesting her. I remained calm and asked, "Why do you not want to go home? Who do you live with? She responded, "I live with my dad and his new wife. She has two boys and they are mean to me." I began to see the tears develop in her eyes. I asked, "Why are they mean to you? What do they do to you?" She replied, "I don't know why they are mean to me. They beat me up all the time. I try to go in my room, but they push the door open and come in anyway. They hold me down and punch and kick me."

She raised her pant leg up to show me a bruise on her leg. She also had one on her arm. I felt the rage inside of me increase as if I were a thermometer stuck inside a hot roast coming out of an oven with the red line slowly moving toward the top. I had got attached to her in my own little way because she had her own way of asking me for things and getting help with my tests. It is so amazing how you do not miss anything until it is gone. People do not realize how much they actually did pay attention to something or someone until they are no longer around!!!

My next question was important. I had to be careful how I asked it because I did not want her to get scared and walk out of my office. I got up and went to sit in the chair beside her. She still had her head down. I looked at her and asked, "Heather when your stepbrothers come in your room and jump on you, do they touch you in a bad way?" She raised her head and said, "No ma'am. They don't do anything like that. All they do is kick and punch me." I let out a big sigh of relief and said, "Okay sweetie. Have you told anyone else this? Have you told your dad?" She said, "I don't hardly get to see him. When he is at home, he is with my stepmom. I haven't told anyone what they do to me, but you Coach."

My eyes began to tear up once she said that, but I refused to let those tears roll down my face. I felt helpless. I wanted to rescue her and get her away from that house, but I could not do that. I had to follow proper protocol for situations like that. I asked, "Do you go to church Heather?" She replied, "No ma'am. We don't go, but I wish we did." I asked, "Is there anything that you have that you really love and cherish? It may be a book, teddy bear, a rock, a swing, a tree, or something like that." She responded, "I like to collect rocks that have different designs on them. I have a lot of them." I said, "When you go home, get those rocks and keep them close to you. I want you to use them as your protector from anything or anyone you think may hurt you. Take one or two of them out and keep with you at all times." She finally looked up at me with those droopy brown eyes and said, "Okay coach I will. Thank you for listening to me." I said, "You are very welcome. Is it okay if I pray with you right now?" She said, "Okay." We stood and joined hands as I began to pray:

> "Dear Heavenly Father, first and foremost of our lives, thank you for waking us up this morning and guiding us throughout our day. Father, Heather needs you right now more than ever. Her stepbrothers need you even more. Touch their spirits and ask them to stop bullying their stepsister. I ask that you put your arms around her as a shield of protection from any harm that may come her way. Please touch and allow me to be there for her the best way possible. In your name I do pray, Amen." I gave her a big hug, and said, "I love you, and if you need to talk about anything my door will always be open."

I called her dad for the rest of that week. I finally got in touch with him after three days. I explained who I was and proceeded to let him know why I was calling. These were his words, "Coach I appreciate you for calling to let me know what's going on with my daughter, but Heather is known for telling lies. True enough her and the boys do have their arguments from time to time, but it's no different than any other sibling fighting. It's harmless."

I could not believe what I was hearing. I took a deep breath to calm myself down because my initial response was to cuss him the hell out. I wanted badly to ask him how he could not at least believe his daughter, his blood daughter! I calmly said, "Thank you for talking with me sir. Can you please talk to Heather and the boys and see what's going on? Let me know if there is anything else I can do sir." I never heard anything else from him.

A few weeks had passed. Heather came in my office to borrow some shorts. As I was getting them for her, I asked, "How are things going at home?" She slowly said, "They stopped for a while coach, but then started back being mean to me and beating me up again. I got my rocks and I have been doing what you told me to. It's helping some coach. They do not be mean to me as much as they use to. My rocks protect me." She left out after that. I was furious inside.

CHAPTER 17

Marianna

*Children are bullied by parents every day, but most of society
does not know because children will not dare report it.*

Marianna was in the eighth grade my first year teaching. She was in my first period class. She was short, with long hair. She wore blue-gray contacts. She looked just like POCHAHONTAS. She made all A's and always had a smile that lit up a room. She was one of those pretty girls who did not too much care for sports. She was smart enough to not get an F in PE though. She dressed out, but during class she just stood there. She moved around, but if the ball came her way, she just moved out of the way.

I was passing out their test one Friday. When I got to her, she had tears in her eyes. She did not speak like she usually do. Her face was swollen. I asked, "What's wrong sweetie?" It was as if I was not standing there because she did not respond. I said, "Stop by my office once you get dressed." Still looking ahead as if she was out in space, she said, "okay." I continued passing out tests.

She walked into my office. I said, "Have a seat." As she sat down, she began to tell me what was going on. She dated the best athlete at the school, Tevin. He was African-American. She did not get to attend many of Tevin's games. She explained, "The reason I'm upset coach is because of my dad. He keep me under lock and key. We had a huge argument last night. I just don't understand why he did not let me do anything. I'm a good kid coach. All I do is come to school make good grades, go home take care of my sisters and brother, clean up the house."

She said, "Coach Tevin and I were on the phone as usual that night. My dad just came in the room all of a sudden and snatched the phone out of my hand." "Why did he do that?" I asked. She said, "He was in one of his moods and tripping hard." Then all of a sudden she dropped her head and allowed the tears to fall like rain in the month of April. It was extremely hard for me to see Marianna in that element because she was always the one in a good mood. She never appeared to have any problems.

These were her words, "None of the girls at this school like me coach, especially the black girls because of Tevin. They think he should be with a black girl and not a Mexican. I just can't take it anymore. I don't do anything to them. On top of all of that my dad attacks me verbally. He has always done it, but it's getting worse. I'm too scared to say anything as far as how he makes me feel because he will beat me with whatever he can get his hands on." I knew what I should have done, but Marianna must have known what I was thinking. She lifted her head quickly and said, "Coach please don't say anything to nobody cause he will kill me! I have to be home to protect my brothers and sisters." I asked, "Do you go to church?" She replied,

"Sometimes, but not as much as I would like to." I walked over to her and gave her a big hug. She was the first student I hugged who was shorter than me. ☺ I asked, "Can I pray with you?" She said, "Okay. Sure." We bowed our heads as I began to pray:

> "Dear Heavenly Father, first and foremost of our lives. Thank you for waking us and guiding us throughout our day. Father Marianna and I stand here asking you to please protect her and her family. Open her dad's eyes to see that he has great children whom he can trust and allow to do things as well as enjoy being a teenager. Give him the wisdom to communicate with his children instead of reacting all of the time. As always give me strength and wisdom to be here for Marianna and give her the best advice possible. In your name I pray, Amen."

A few weeks went by and I began to notice the old Marianna was back. I asked her to stop by my office after she got dressed. She came in my office and took a seat. She had that big, beautiful smile that I had not seen in a while. I looked at her and said, "I assume that things are going better at home." She smiled before responding, "Yeah coach, everything is fine. My dad calmed down, but it won't be long before he snap out again. I just hope I can come and talk to you when it happens again. I just need to let it out sometimes coach. I know it is not good to hold things in. Thank you coach. My cousin told me you were a good person and that I could trust you. She was right."

CHAPTER 18

Star

When a child gets bullied because of their weight if affects their self-esteem.

Bullying was very evident during PE class in terms of children getting tortured because of their weight. I lectured on bullying children who are overweight almost every day. I had sympathy for all of the students who came to me with problems, but it tore me to pieces when a child came to me because they were getting bullied because of their weight. I was hurt to the core when I realized students would rather fail PE by not dressing out because of their weight than deal with the torture and humiliation from their peers.

Star was a very intellectual young lady. I had the pleasure of meeting her my second year teaching. She was in the seventh grade. She was Caucasian with shoulder length brown hair. She was a little taller than me. She came from a good family who definitely made sure she had everything she needed to be successful in life. She had a good sense of fashion because the girl could dress. She loved getting her nails and toes done. She was shy and quiet. She had one close friend, Amanda, who she referred to as her "bestie."

Amanda was overweight as well. She was Caucasian with long blonde hair. They were about the same height. Amanda was far from shy. She was intelligent as well. She was definitely the kind of person who set her own trend and followed her own path. She reminded me of the actor Monique. Every day she walked in the gym for class she always found me and said, "Morning coach. The queen is in the building. I'm big, beautiful, and loving it baby!" I always had a mean look on my face to let the children know they were not going to run over me, but hearing Amanda make her grand entrance daily, I could not help but smile. Her and Star were inseparable.

Star dressed out on a regular basis. Due to the fact that she was very smart, sometimes she dressed out and just stood on the floor amongst the class. A few weeks before Thanksgiving break, she did not dress out. She always stuck her head in my office to speak and ask how my day was going. During that week she did not dress out, she did not say anything to anybody. Surprisingly, Amanda continued to dress out and participate.

If ever the children did not dress out, they were not allowed to go to the locker room or anything. They were to sit in the bleachers at the very top. Their book bags were to remain on my side of the gym until class was dismissed. They were not to talk, do homework, or read a book! The girls sat in one section. The boys sat in another section. I gave zeroes for not dressing out at least that is what the children thought. I gave them a fifty. It never failed at the end of the year how children came to my office crying, begging, and pleading for ways to pull their grade up to passing. If they came to me on their own, I most definitely found something for them to do for extra credit. Sometimes I had them cleaning the gym, my office, or writing a book report.

After class, I asked Star to come to my office. She walked in with her head down. I was sitting at my desk going through my grade book. I did not raise my head to look at her. As I wrote grades down I began to talk: "Star I noticed you have not been dressing out during class. Up until now you had an A. What are you going to do about that?" She sat motionless in front of my desk with her head down. Her hands were clenched together on her lap. She responded, "I don't know and don't care."

I could not believe what I was seeing or hearing. She had this I don't care attitude. I knew something was seriously wrong. I closed my grade book and moved my chair beside hers. We both just sat their quiet for a minute. Finally I said, "Whenever you are ready to talk I will be here. As a matter of fact I am going to send a note to your next period teacher to ask if it's okay for you to be with me." I went to Coach Harrington's class to get a student to take the note to Star's teacher.

When I walked back in my office she was crying. I calmly sat down back beside her. I grabbed some paper towels off of my desk and handed them to her. I said, "Whatever is going on, you can tell me. I'm right here with you. We can figure out a solution to the problem together."

Still crying, she said, "Coach I'm a nice person who treats people the way I want to be treated. I help people when they need help. I'm a good kid who respects my parents and everything. I absolutely love your class and the way you teach. Before you came I never set foot on that gym floor to play anything. You make sure we have fun and learn along the way as long as we follow the rules. My self-esteem has always been low cause of my weight coach, but I put a smile on my face and keep it moving. I know things will get better. You are the reason for that. I look at you and all you have been through. You give me hope. I try to lose weight and eat right, but it's hard. I cry myself to sleep almost every night cause of my weight. I come from a family who loves to eat. My dad is overweight and a diabetic. My mom can eat whatever she wants and barely gains weight. That makes it hard for me to turn down food that she cooks. My dad's family is big. The men look like big football players and the women are not far from it. I want to put an end to obesity when I have children. I just do not know what to do coach."

She started crying harder. I put my arms around her shoulder and said, "I can help create a diet and exercise plan just for you. It's not going to be easy, but with hard work, determination, and dedication I know you can do it." She continued, "Coach I need something right now. I'm tired of people making fun of and picking on me cause of my weight. I thought about committing suicide this week." I sat straight up, looked at her, and said, "Who making fun of you? When do they pick on you? Why haven't you said something?"

I was furious and my protective instincts automatically kicked in. Her tears began to dry up. She cleared her throat and responded, "Coach it is not a particular person. It's a little of everybody. That's why I have not been participating in your class. The girls talk about me in the locker room when I get dressed. The boys do not want me on their team cause they say I'm too *fat* to play. Coach those remarks hurt my feelings so bad."

She said, "Coach I know you love us and will do anything for us. I know you take bullying seriously and for that reason I am not gonna tell you the names of who says mean things about me. Instead can you do something else for me?" At that very moment my eyes filled with liquid. I responded, "What's that?" She said, "Just have a talk with everybody as a whole. They just say those things to fit in with everybody else. Ten years from now they won't even remember being this cruel."

I could not believe how caring and considerate she was. I saw so much of my character in her. I could not help but think, "This is going to be a very productive adult when she enters the real world. Wow! She is definitely going to do something with her life." I had to turn away to quickly wipe the tears from my eyes before she seen them. "Coach I just want to have confidence in myself like Amanda. She is beautiful and has self-esteem as if she is a super model. I'm just ugly. The boys I like don't like me back. None of the other girls will invite me to sleep overs or parties."

I said, "You have the one thing that I never had growing up. I'm pretty sure your peers don't have it either and that's *Amanda*. She is really a good friend to you. I know she defends you because I hear her. Good friends are hard to find." She responded, "I know coach and I thank God for her every day."

"You feel better now that you have gotten all of that of your chest? Next week I can expect to see you back on the floor having fun with PE right?" By that time her body language was positive as well as her facial expression. She looked at me with those big brown eyes and said, "Of course."

I walked over gave her a big hug and asked, "May I pray with you?" She replied, "Would you please." We joined hands, bowed our heads, and I began:

"Dear Heavenly Father, first and foremost of our lives thank you so much for waking us this morning and watching over us throughout this glorious day. Here standing before me is a very remarkable young lady who I know in my heart is going to be very successful in the future. Right now the devil is riding her back putting negative thoughts into her mind. He is also putting negative thoughts in her peers' minds to say to her. I ask at this very moment that you not only put your protective shield around Star, but around them as well. They know not what they do Jesus and you are the only one who has the power to put an end to it. Please keep Star around positive people and give her the strength she needs to fight gluttony. I thank you for blessing me to be here for her. As long as you see fit, I will continue to be here for her. I also pray for her family. Help her to stay on the right path and have faith in you that everything will be okay and that she will reap a harvest soon. In your name I pray, Amen."

CHAPTER 19

Recognizing Class Individuality

As a teacher, it becomes clear to notice certain characteristics about different groups as they are promoted throughout each year.

My last year teaching was unbelievable. I learned to look at each class as a whole from the sixth grade to the eighth grade. They were supposed to improve individually, academically, intellectually, physically, spiritually, emotionally, and socially, as they got older. By the time they made it to the eighth grade, it was clear to see what type of personality they were going to have once they got to the high school.

On occasion I spoke to the sixth grade teachers to get a better understanding of the students I encountered to see what level they were on. Their response was either, "Coach they are a *good* group or Coach they are a *bad* group. Be prepared for anything!" During my first year, the eighth grade class was athletic, academic, responsible, and mature. Their MCT2 scores were outstanding. I did not have any major problems coaching the girls. They listened and were eager to learn. The eighth grade girls' record that year was 10-4. The seventh grade girls' record was 6-2. The eighth grade boys had a perfect season. Their record was 14-0. They made it to the final round in the district championship, but lost by two points.

During my second year, the eighth grade class who were the previous seventh grade class were athletic and capable of performing well in academics, but were just lazy. Either they had book sense and no common sense or common sense and no book sense. In the athletic sense, they had to be told, "Just play ball and do not think!" If they thought during events or games, they were not that successful. The older they got, the worse they got. The girls' basketball record that season was 5-10, the same girls who had a 6-2 record the previous year. Some of them just did not comprehend what was taught in any subject. Their MCT2 scores were not good at all.

During my third and final year the eighth grade class was unbelievable. The things they did were just unimaginable. They had the worst attitudes. They did not listen. They stayed in trouble. They were very disrespectful and rude. They were bullies and very mean. Surprisingly, they were exceptionally good in academics. They were just a group who wanted to do their own thing no matter what, by any means necessary. The eighth grade girls' record was 4-11. The seventh grade girls' basketball record was 7-3. The eighth grade girls did not come to basketball camp. They did not put forth any effort during games. I chewed them out after every game. I ran them hard during practice, but they still did not care. They wanted to have a winning season true enough, but were not willing to do what they had to in order to earn it! They cared more about the boys and their appearance on the court. They literally were in games on the court, staring in the stands at the boys.

The sixth grade class was something I had never seen before my final year as well. They gave the definition of bullying a new meaning. They were BULLIES from hell. Some of them were bullies because they were just mean and wanted to torment others. Some of them were bullies because they had to toughen up and defend themselves. Either way, in the classroom the teachers caught hell. It was hard to teach and introduce lessons plans while having to deal with bullying issues.

It was even harder in the gym to teach PE. They argued and fussed about everything. The PE department always monitored the students in the hallway, locker rooms, and gymnasium, but we had to create a new strategy every week just about. I had parent after parent coming to the school because of an incident that occurred in the gym concerning their child due to bullying. It was nerve racking. It got to the point where parents showed up and sat in the gym during class watching their child. They also were watching how we taught, monitored, and handled situations concerning the students.

CHAPTER 20

The Fight Club

Cyberbullying is done through the use of electronics. It uses instant messages, text messages, cell phones, and online networks to humiliate a person.

My last year teaching bullying was extremely prevalent. The eighth graders had a major effect on the sixth and seventh graders. Bullying began to show in extracurricular activities as well. I did not allow myself to gossip with teachers. Therefore, the only way I knew what was going on was when the kids told me. I never asked them anything. The kids trusted me that much and enjoyed being around me that much. When they came to me about things that were going on between other kids or even teachers for that matter, it was for me to help them. They did not come to me to gossip because they knew I did not care for gossipers. They always said, "Coach what do I do? How can I handle this situation? I was told you give good advice. Please talk to my friend."

I was cleaning out the bleachers and the hallway, something I always did between classes, and three boys walked over to me. I saw them before in PE, but they were in one of the other coaches' class. It was two Caucasians, Justin and William, and one African-American, Darren. I continued cleaning as they began to talk. "Coach Lowery, "May we speak to you in private for a moment please?" I answered, "You sure can." As we entered my office, I sat down and they did as well. Two sat in the chairs and one sat on the floor with his back propped against my computer stand. They looked at each other, took a big breath, and let out a huge sigh. I had no clue what I was about to hear. They kept it short and simple because they did not want to be late for their next class. Darren and William did most of the talking. Justin just looked up every now and then and shook his head in agreement to what the other two said.

Darren and William continued, "Coach we in the sixth grade and we can't wait until next year so we can play football, but we have been hearing rumors." I asked, "What kind of rumors?" "Coach, in the PE locker room, some of the other boys said the football team had a fight club. The seventh graders had to fight the eighth graders. They film the whole thing and send it to other kids. They also pick who is going to fight. The winner gets paid!" I could not believe what I was hearing. Nine times out of ten it was true too. Those boys were scared as hell as they informed me what was going on. I could see the concern in their faces. They were worried someone was going to get severely hurt if not killed! The one question I wanted an answer to was, "Where were all of the coaches when all of this was going on." Football teams have a ton of coaches. How could they not have known the fighting was going on? To make matters worse, it was the end of the season when the fighting was discovered!

The seventh grade boys rubbed off on the sixth grade boys. It became very clear to see during PE. The boys' locker room was a war zone for bullies. The exact same thing that was done to the seventh grade by the eighth grade was being done to the sixth grade. The bullying cycle was taking its course. I decided to step up and resolve as many problems that I could relating to bullying. I always talked to the kids before, during, and after class. If Jesus put something on my heart to tell the kids, I told them.

I was sitting in my office one afternoon preparing for my next class. There was a crack in my door. I did not have it closed all the way. I glanced up and noticed a shadow in the hall. I could tell it was a boy. He stood there trying to decide if he should come in. I sat motionless at my desk as he stood there. Then all of a sudden he dropped his head for about five seconds. He lifted it, took a deep breath, and knocked on the door. I said, "Come in." He was nervous as he stood in the doorway. He slowly took one step and then another. I said, "Have a seat son." I had no clue of who he was. He was not in any of my classes. I had never seen him before. He was Caucasian and short. He had short, dark brown hair and wore glasses.

He sat down and began to rub his hands in a steady motion across his legs. He stared at the floor. He began to express what was on his mind. "Coach Lowery I know you don't know who I am, but I always hear people talking about how you helped them. My name is Jonathan. I'm in the seventh grade. I play football." He began to turn red in the face. He started shaking his head from side to side, but it was not due to nerves. He was mad with rage. I said, "Take a deep breath Jonathan and tell me what's going on." He proceeded, "Coach there is a lot of stuff that goes on the locker room, but we too scared to say anything."

I interrupted him because I automatically assumed he meant the locker room in my gym. The children knew I did not tolerate foolishness in the locker room. I asked, "What kind of things are going on in the locker room in the gym? I will go straighten it out right now!" He said, "It's not happening up here. It's downstairs in the football locker room. The eighth graders pick on us. They mean to us on the field. When they tackle us it hurts like they trying to kill us. We scared to tell the coaches. They tell us they gonna kick our ass if we tell. At first it wasn't so bad, but it got worse a month ago." I said, "How did it get worse?"

As he took another deep breath, I could feel deep in my spirit that I was not going to like what he was about to say. He said, "They make us fight coach in the locker room on game day. They pick an eighth grader and a seventh grader to fight on Monday. We have all week to get ready for the fight on Thursday." Without hesitation, I said, "Where are ya'll coaches at during these fights?" He said, "Outside somewhere. They be making sure everything is prepared for the game."

I remember thinking to myself, "Football gets so much praise, attention, support, and money. They have more coaches than any other sport. How in the hell could they allow something like this to happen? How could it have been going on for so long and no one knew? Why was there not a coach assigned to monitor the players in the locker room?" I asked, "Can you explain how they set up the fights?" Before responding to the question, he said, "Coach I ain't no punk. They think they can be mean and bully us. They think we scared, but I ain't scared. They think cause I'm short that I can't fight. I might get beat up when my turn comes, but I'm gonna fight til it's over coach!" He had his left hand in a fist. The right hand was open. He kept punching the right hand with the left. I said, "I know you're not a punk, but you do not have to fight to prove yourself Jonathan." He began to explain the fighting process.

"On Monday after football practice one name is pulled from two football helmets. One helmet has eighth grade names in it. The other helmet has seventh grade names in it. B.J. pulls from the eighth grade helmet. Cody pulls from the seventh grade helmet. The team gathers around waiting to see who gets called. The eighth graders are excited and ready to beat the crap out of us. We be scared and nervous coach. After the names are called the two fighters meet in the center. Cody stands in the middle, tell the fighters to touch gloves (there are no gloves though), and say "fight."

During the fights Anthony, stands at the door to watch for coaches. Mason films the fight with his phone and forwards it to other kids. Eddie walks around and take money from the team as they bet on who will win. The winner gets the money and earns respect coach. When I fight, I'm gonna win that money!"

I could not believe what I was hearing. I said, "You are not going to have to fight sweetie. I'm glad that you came to me. I'm going to do what I can to fix the problem." He said, "Okay. Please don't tell that I told you cause they will call me a snitch and beat me up coach." I leaned forward in my chair and said, "I NEVER reveal my sources when ya'll come talk to me. You can trust me." He stood up and said, "Thank you coach for listening to me. I'm glad I came to you."

For the remainder of the day I contemplated the next step I should take. I wanted to handle the situation properly without revealing my source. More importantly, I wanted to resolve the bullying situation. I had to find a way to get the kids to understand how they should not do that. Someone else must have gotten tired and worried as well because by the time seventh period began rumors were floating around. I noticed the principals standing outside in a huddle. Seventh period was when I had the eighth grade girls' basketball team. As they were running down the hall to the locker room, I heard them talking as usual. They ran because they had five minutes after the tardy bell rung to be dressed and on the floor. If they did not, they had to run. They hated running. ☺

From time to time I stood at the door as they got dressed listening to their conversation. My office was adjacent to the locker room. As I stood there, I heard them whispering, "I can't believe the football team would do something so stupid. Why would they fight each other? Where the coaches be at? I feel so sorry for the seventh graders. I'm glad we got Coach Lowery as our coach. We should tell her so she can help. She always there for us. I know she will do all she can for them too."

I always got emotional when it came down to my girls. I could not believe how much they listened to me and respected me. I cleared my throat before entering the locker room to give them a heads up that I was walking in. After discussing the agenda for the day, I asked, "Did ya'll know about the fighting going on downstairs in the football locker room?" They lifted their heads quickly and replied, "No coach! We would've told you if we did because you always tell us that we are a family on this basketball team. We should treat our teammates like they are our sisters. Sisters don't suppose to fight like that coach. They not acting like a team should act."

The next day I found Mason, Cody, B.J., Anthony, and Eddie. Mason Hilton was African-American. He was in the eighth grade. He was tall and dark. His body frame was average with the exception of his developing muscles. His hair was long and he kept it braided. He had a lot of respect from his peers. Cody was Caucasian. He had a real nice tan. He was average height and skinny. He was in the seventh grade. He wore his hair in a Mohawk. He was definitely a follower. He did what he seen everyone else do. B.J. was Caucasian. He was tall with developing muscles as well. His hair was short and blonde. He was in the eighth grade. The girls loved him. He came from a very wealthy family who was well known in the community. Anthony was African-American. He was short with average body size. He kept a low neat haircut. He actually was quiet. He kept to himself. He was in the seventh grade. Eddie was African-American. He was tall with a bright skin complexion. His hair was dreaded up. He was in the grade. He got in trouble from time to time, but no more than what was expected of children his age.

I knew B.J., Cody, and Eddie because they took PE. Mason and Anthony did not take PE, but they knew who and how I was. All five of them were nervous and scared. I sat down at my desk and calmly looked at them. My door was open as usual when I had students in my office. I began to speak, "Do ya'll know why I called you in my office?" Two of them were sitting and the other three were standing. I only had two chairs in my office. They all were staring at the floor and responded, "No ma'am?" I said, "Ya'll raise your heads and look at me. I'm gonna ask one more time. Do ya'll know why I called you in my office?"

Cody responded, "Because of the fighting." I said, "I don't know exactly who started it or how it started. The only thing I'm upset about is someone could've seriously got hurt. I can't stand bullies and this has bullying written all over it. I know what it's like to be bullied." I told them about my experiences with bullying. The more I talked, the more their body language showed regret. Eddie said, "Coach you got picked on? I would have never thought you got bullied?" The others shook their head in agreement to Eddie's response.

When I finished telling them my story I stood up and propped my back on the wall. I could see the fear in their eyes. They did not know what I was about to do. I stared them in the eyes and said, "I do not know what the school is going to do as far as punishing the team. I know everything. I know who took money, who was watching the door, who started the fights, who drew names from helmets, and who filmed the fights. I'm willing to do whatever I have to for you all to understand how bad this is. You should not bully anyone, especially your teammates! There is a prison fifteen minutes away from here. If I have to, I will get permission, put ya'll on a bus and take you to visit the inmates. Doing something like this and continuing down the wrong path is going to lead you to jail anyway. You might as well see where you are going to be living."

They did not move or say anything after I said that. They were scared. I asked, "Do ya'll want to go to jail?" They shook their heads no. I said, "No matter what anyone else has told you. I believe in you and expect nothing but the best from you. If you can create a "street fighting" tournament and actually get an entire team involved, then you all are *LEADERS*. Instead of leading people in a negative direction, try leading them in a positive direction. I am very disappointed in you."

They looked shocked that I said that. I wrote them hall passes and told them to go back to class. As they were walking out Cody said, "Coach I don't know what I was thinking. My grandma always tell me what you just said about being a leader. I'm gonna try and do better coach for you and my grandma." I looked at him and said, "Don't do better for us. Do better for YOU!" It took a while, but I assumed the principals got down to the root of the problem.

CHAPTER 21

Bullying Because of Sexuality

*Homosexual children and teens are bullied at an
outstanding rate, which sometimes lead to suicide.*

Homosexuality is going to be a part of society whether people accept it or not. Homosexuality is not hidden anymore. No one wants to speak on the subject, especially in the education field, because they fear what people may think and they also fear they may lose their job. Everyone either has a gay person in their family, on their jobs, or in their friend circle whether they accept it or not. It is not always about accepting gays, it is about *RESPECTING* the lifestyle. It is no different than respecting people who live together and are not married (shacking), or people who have babies out of wedlock, or anything else for that matter because there are a ton of things that society has grown to respect that are not approved of in the *GOOD BOOK!*

One of the hardest things in the world is for a parent to learn that their child is gay. It is also hard for a teacher to learn a student is gay. I was very surprised when I learned that I taught many homosexual kids. They were not ashamed to let people know they were gay, especially the girls. Teachers need to understand that. I took it upon myself to become educated about teaching children who are homosexual. I could not believe some of the information I discovered. Homosexual teenagers commit suicide at a higher rate. They not only have to face bullies on a daily basis, but also have to come to terms with the fact that they are gay. That is enough to deal with alone itself. There were more girls to talk to me about their sexuality than boys. The girls did not deal with bullies as much as the boys did. Gay girls were accepted by their peers more than the gay boys. I did not understand that concept at all.

I actually caught two girls kissing in the hallway during my student teaching internship at a high school. They were very open with their relationship. Everyone at the school knew. I was amazed at how their peers accepted them as they walked down the hall or sat together in the cafeteria. I told my supervising teacher, Coach Hill, what I seen. She informed me that I had to write them up because it was a form of PDA, public display of affection. I did just that. Later on during the week we received a visit from the parent of one of the girls. She wanted a conference with Coach Hill, the principal, and me. She was furious because "I was lying," she said. "My child is not gay! I would know if she was," she yelled.

Her daughter was a senior and a good kid. She was on the track team. She performed well in all of her events. She dressed like a boy. She wore baggy jeans with boy shirts and boy shoes. She walked like a boy and everything. How could her mom not ask herself if her daughter was gay? In situations like that it only told me one of two things: 1) the parent(s) was in denial or 2) the parent (s) was blind and could not see it. How could a person carry a child nine months, give birth, raise that child for eighteen years in their home, and not question their sexuality? As a teacher I recognized kids who I could pretty much see were gay or going to be gay!

When I started doing research on gay children and teens in schools, things became clear to me. I have never been much of a "Lifetime" person when it comes to television networks. Honestly, I have never watched television that much. One day I was flipping through the channels and a movie, *"A Prayer for Bobby"* came on Lifetime. Seeing as to how I am very spiritual, the title alone captivated me. I will never forget that movie. Basically it was about a young man who came from a very religious family. He had a girlfriend throughout high school, but realized his senior year that something was not right. He told his family he was gay and OMG!

His mom started praying for him and leaving sticky notes with bible scriptures on them all over the house. He moved out of the house after graduating high school to another state. He was happy and dating men for a while, but could not be totally happy because his family did not accept his sexuality or better yet respect it! One night he walked to the top of a bridge and jumped. His suicide destroyed his family, especially his mom.

After his death, she took it upon herself to educate as many parents that she could on raising a gay child. She supported groups and parades for gays, but she beat herself up for a long time because of how she treated him when he was alive. I will never understand that. "You don't miss your water until your well runs dry. You don't realize what you had until it's gone." Why does life work like that? The movie was based on a true story.

I have a gay aunt. I have not seen her since I was a kid. Growing up she was my favorite Tee Tee. I idolized her independency. She married a man and moved to another state. That was the last time I saw her. A few months after being married, she realized that was not for her, at least not with a man!! The sad thing is no one knows her exact location. Her older brother died in 2002 and we could not even contact her to inform her about the funeral. I doubt she would have come anyway. This aunt is on my dad's side of the family. She is the baby girl of sixteen children. My mom, her youngest brother, Uncle Stokes, and one of my cousins are the only people who communicate with her and know where she lives.

My mom went to visit her when I was 14. I remember her calling once momma made it home to check on her. Momma gave me the phone. She said, "How ya'll been doing?" I said, "Okay, ready for the summer." She went on about how much fun her and mom had. Then all of a sudden out of nowhere, she said, "Your mom told you I was gay right." I said, "Yeah she told me." She asked, "You okay with that?" I said, "Yeah as long as you happy." That was that.

I did not really think about why she never came home to visit until I turned 19 or 20. She was probably embarrassed and did not want her family to see her in her new lifestyle. Maybe she did not want people staring or pointing at her. Maybe she did not want to be bothered with the gossip. Maybe she wondered if we would accept her sexuality. A million questions went through my mind and still do. How many of the children who commit suicide because of bullying are gay? What is the percentage of gay children who deal with bullying? Has bullying increased in the last ten years? These are serious questions to think about.

CHAPTER 22

Billy

The effects of bullying because of sexuality can lead to extreme fighting as a means to defend oneself.

I had the pleasure of meeting Billy my last year teaching. He was African-American and tall. He was average size for a boy his age. He failed the seventh grade. He hung around more girls than boys. Every day he came to my class he always ran to me trying to gossip about stuff going on amongst the kids. He could not wait to run his mouth. He was in a fight at least once a month. He stood his ground though. He did not let anyone walk over him. Of all the bully situations I dealt with as a teacher, his had to be the worst. I felt bad because for the first time I did not know how to approach the bullies. I took on the challenge the best way that I could because that's how important it was to me to be a part of the solution to stop bullying.

Billy was in my class first period. He got into a fight one afternoon. He was suspended for three days. I decided to pull him to the side when he returned to school. He had a heart of gold. His grandma was raising him. It was toward the end of the school term and I was teaching activities relating to track. That particular week I took the class outside to do relays around the track field. I walked around with the class as well. I asked Billy to walk with me. As we walked the conversation began.

I said, "Billy why did you get suspended?" He said, "Coach Lowery I got to fighting again. I'm tired of people picking on me. They think I'm soft and can't fight, but I will beat they ass." He looked at me quickly and covered his mouth because he realized he cursed.

He said, "Oops my bad coach. I meant beat they butt." I asked, "Why do they pick on you? Who picks on you?" He responded, "It mostly be boys. They call me a sissy, a faggit, and a punk. They pick on me cause I'm gay." What he said next touched me to the core.

We began walking slowly. He said, "Coach you have no idea what it's like to be gay. I go to church almost every Sunday with my grandma. I love to sing in the choir. I actually listen to the message our pastor preach to us. I'm a good person. Do you think I chose to be gay? Would I really be gay on purpose and put myself through the torture I get from people at this school? I cry myself to sleep almost every night because I have to defend myself every day I come to school."

All I could say was, "Things will get better. Just hold on and keep the faith. Later on in your life you will see what I meant when I said everything you do comes back on you. I know you have to defend yourself when they pick on you like that, but I want you to do one thing for me." He looked at me and said, "What Coach Lowery?" I said, "I want you to stop fighting so much. I know you have to defend yourself, but try and walk away. Unless someone puts their hands on you, don't fight. People are going to always talk and say bad things about you. You need to decide if you are going to give them the power over *YOUR* life. I know it hurts you and make you mad when they say bad things about you, but try to ignore it. You do not need to miss any more days from school. You can always come talk to me. I may not understand, but I will always listen." He said, "Yes ma'am.

He ran to catch up to the group of girls he always walk with, but before he took off he turned toward me and said, "Coach everybody told me you was mean and I wasn't gonna like you, but you the nicest teacher I know. When you not in one of your moods of course. I have been at this school for two years and you the only person who has talked to me about fighting. Thanks Coach. You my favorite teacher and the best teacher. I don't care what nobody else say."

CHAPTER 23

Zachary

Children are bullied and treated different because they have homosexual parents. Is it their fault that their biological parent(s) refused to step up to the plate and be a devoted parent?

I had the pleasure of meeting Zachary (Zach) my second year teaching in 2008-2009. He was in the seventh grade. He was Caucasian and about six feet tall. He was in my second period class. He did not get in any trouble. He was an overall good kid. He had gorgeous blonde hair. It was short and smooth. It was clear to see that he came from a good home and had good ethical and moral values. He was not a quiet kid, but neither was he loud.

I started teaching Health that year as well. I enjoyed getting the kids involved as much as possible. Class discussions were a must in my room. I incorporated journal entries as well. I wrote a topic sentence on the board every morning. Once the children came to class, they were to get their journals, write on the topic, and turn it in once they finished. I only gave them ten minutes to complete the assignment. It allowed me to check roll and set up other assignments that I may have forgotten, which I rarely did because I am what one might call an over achiever. I arrived at work thirty minutes early every day to prepare lessons. I left work ten or fifteen minutes after we got off.

The kids trusted me with reading their journals. I am not too sure what the topic was one particular day, but Zach's journal entry touched my soul. I learned that his parents were lesbians. They adopted him from birth. He wrote how he was fortunate to have good parents who loved and cared for him. His biological mother was on drugs the duration of her pregnancy. What was an eye opener for me was the fact that he got bullied by Max because he had gay parents.

Max was in the seventh grade, but he was supposed to be in the tenth grade. He was a big bully anyway. He was Caucasian, but thought he was African-American! He sounded black when he talked. Most of the teachers were scared of him, but I had no problem with him. He wore glasses with a short haircut. His hair was light brown.

The more I read Zach's journal, the angrier I became. I had always heard stories on television dealing with children getting bullied because their parents were gay, but I guess I never thought I would one day face a situation similar to it. Toward the end of Zach's journal entry he wrote, "Coach Lowery always tell us to RESPECT people no matter who or what they are. I try, but sometimes it's just too hard. She tell us we may not understand a person's religion, race, gender, sexuality, and so forth, but when we enter the real world, we are going to meet all kinds of people. We are going to have to work with them, go to church with them, and interact with them in many other ways. She always tell us to treat people the way we want to be treated." I knew what I had to do, but was not sure how to do it. I prayed about it for a week asking Jesus to show me what to do.

Tuesday of the next week Zach came to my office before class. He knocked quietly and came in and sat down. There was silence for about three minutes. Then he began to speak, "Coach Lowery I know I should probably be in the counselor's office for what I am about to say, but I feel more comfortable talking to you. You always tell us how you were bullied growing up. I have been getting picked on by Max. At first I over looked him and tried to not stoop to his level like you tell us to do, but that's not working anymore."

I asked, "How long has he been picking on you? Why is he picking on you?" He took a deep breath and said, "He been doing it for two months. He pick on me cause I have gay parents. He call me, "the future faggit." He say things like, "Zach gonna be gay cause his parents are gay and that somebody gonna take his booty." Or if we changing clothes in the locker room, he tell the boys, "Ya'll better turn ya'll back cause Zach might try to suck your dick."

I could not believe what I was hearing. Zach was getting angry as he sat there. I asked, "When he makes those comments what do you do?" He replied, "Nothing. I ignore him." I asked, "Do he try to fight you?" He said, "No ma'am, but I'm tired Coach. I'm a nice person and I may have to moms as parents true enough, but I love them. They have done everything to make sure I have a good life. Max think I'm weak, but I'm gonna show him."

I calmly said, "Take a deep breath Zach and unball your fist. You are a good kid who makes excellent grades. You do not get in trouble. You are very respectable and well-mannered. I am not going to tell you to walk up and fight Max, but I will say this because I tell my little sisters the same thing. As long as he don't touch you don't worry about it, but if he put his hands on you, you fight back. You have every right to defend yourself. Both of ya'll are going to get suspended, but you will not get as many days as he will. Now don't leave out of here saying I told you to fight because that's not what I'm saying." He responded, "Yes ma'am. I know what you mean." I asked, "Have you told your parents about Max?"

He sat up as if a cold chill went down his spine and said, "Oooh no Coach. One of my mom's is nice and logical, but the other one is crazy. She don't think before she react. She will come up here and blow the school up. I don't want her to go to jail. Besides they already have enough to deal with and I do not want to put any more problems on them." I could not help but laugh after he said that. ☺ Then I thought to myself, "This is a pretty amazing kid. Most kids could care less about the stress their parents deal with!"

Zach played soccer and he admitted that he was not the best player on the team, but it meant the world to him when his parents came to watch him play. I leaned forward placing my elbows on my desk and said, "Let me talk to Max first before you do something you will regret." He said, "Okay, but please hurry Coach cause I can't ignore him anymore." I asked, "Do ya'll go to church?" Smiling he said, "Of course we do Coach. We got the best pastor in the world. I actually listen to him. The same things you tell us are the same things he preach about." I smiled back and stood up. I asked, "Is it okay if we pray?" He said, "Yes ma'am." With my short self, I looked like those kids in the movie *"Honey I Shrunk The Kids"* when they were lost in the back yard as I stood next to him. We joined hands and bowed our heads:

> "Dear Heavenly Father, first and foremost of our lives thank you for waking us up this morning and watching over us as we journeyed throughout the day. Father, thank you so much for guiding Zach to me. He needs your help. Please put your arms around him as protection from bullies. Thank you so much for giving him great parents. I pray for Max as well. Touch him Father and take away all the meanness he shows towards Zach and others. When Zach is faced with adversity give him the strength and wisdom to allow *YOU* to be his forefront. Thank you for giving me the opportunity to meet such a talented young man and be a blessing to his life. In your name I pray. Amen."

He bent down to hug me. I said, "Everything will be okay just let Jesus handle it and trust that he will protect you."

Max was in my second period class. He did not give me any trouble, but I knew the younger kids were scared of him. After checking roll, starting class and the activity for the day, I asked the other PE teachers to watch my class for a few minutes. I called Max to my office. Every day he walked into the gym and said, "What's up Coach Loowweerry!" I set up the equipment or cleaned the gym until the kids were in their roll call seats. I did not even make eye contact as he walked by and spoke. On that particular day my response was, "What's up Max. After I check roll I need you to go to my office."

When he walked in my office the last thing he thought was that he was in trouble. He sat down and I began, "What grade are you supposed to be in? How old are you? Who do you live with?"

He answered, "I'm sixteen and I suppose to be in the tenth grade. I live with my grandma coach." Before I could continue he asked, "Coach you don't like me do you?" I said, "Why you say that?" He said, "You act mean toward me. You don't say anything to me in class. You don't call on me to be team captain or ask me to do stuff in the gym."

My response was, "I wouldn't say I don't like you. I just don't too much care for your character at times. I'm always watching Max especially when you think I'm not. When ya'll get dressed in the boys locker room what else goes on in there?" He replied, "Nothing really. We joke around and clown each other sometimes. Other than, that nothing." I said, "I'm not stupid. I know other things go on in that locker room. What I can't understand is why don't you older boys start being role models for the younger boys? You are too old to act the way you do sometimes. You know that you have a reputation at this school huh? No one wants to be bothered with you Max. My first year here I was told to be prepared for you because you were "bad" and going to give me trouble, but I give every kid a chance to prove themselves to me."

By then he was sitting on the edge of the chair with his head down. His elbows were resting on his knees as his forearm and hands were clenched and hanging. He said, "I know no one likes me as far as teachers go. I can't say I blame them coach. I have made some bad decisions and terrible mistakes. I don't put forth the effort in class cause it's too late. I'm already two grades behind."

I continued, "A young man came to me and informed me that he gets picked on almost every day in the locker room by you mostly. Do you know anything about that?" He said, "Naw Coach." I was sitting in my chair at the desk calm and very relaxed. I leaned forward and said, "Look at me. Lift your head. Do you pick on anybody in the locker room? Think long and hard before you answer cause I want you to tell the truth."

Finally he said, "We all crack jokes on this boy, Zach. We just be playing coach." I said, "What kind of jokes do you say?" He said, "We say he gay cause he got two moms." I stopped him before he went any further and said, "Stop saying we because you are the only one in my office!" He continued, "I tell the boys to cover up and not get dressed in front of him cause he might try to look at them. He gay and like boys."

I interrupted him because I did not want to hear anymore. I was filled with rage. He could tell too. He said, "Coach I don't know what I was thinking. Trying to fit in and be popular I guess. I never thought he took it that serious." I said, "Max if someone said all of that to you how would you feel? Everybody is not as outspoken as you are. Then you are older and a tall, big guy. Do you think Zach really would have told you to leave him alone and that you were hurting his feelings? Why would you say bad things about his parents anyway? Just because he has gay parents doesn't mean that he is gay?"

By then he was sitting back in his chair with his hands on top of his head. His hands were joined together on the center of his head and his elbows stuck out. His body language showed regret. He replied, "I never looked at it like that coach. I wasn't trying to hurt his feelings. I was joking like everybody else. I don't know coach."

I continued, "Now you know I'm upset and the last thing I like is a bully. The first thing you gonna do is apologize to Zach and you better mean it! The next thing you need to decide is do you want my punishment or a write up? You know you don't have too many more times to get in trouble and you're gonna be expelled or kicked out of the school permanently." He leaned forward, contemplating. He finally said, "Man, I'm gonna take your punishment coach."

I stood and began rambling around in my office folding uniforms and things to that nature. I always did that to make whoever was in my office think about what they had done or fill my wrath. Silence was sometimes the best answer. They never knew where my mind was when I ignored them or I was silent. I could hear him breathing heavy and sighing as if he was embarrassed. I could not believe it. I expected a totally different reaction about the entire situation. There were only *THREE* janitors responsible for cleaning the school. We were lucky if we saw one in the gym once a week. I took it upon myself to keep it clean and sometimes got some help.

I said, "Every day you come to the gym you need to push mop the floor before and after class. Pick trash up out of the bleachers. Make sure the trash is taken out of the garbage can and clean the boy's locker room. Do you think you can handle that?" He said, "Yes ma'am." I turned around, looked at him, and said, "Max what do you want to do with your life? Where do you see yourself in ten years? Do you ever wonder how much stress you put on your grandma? She seems to be the only one who cares about you. I know she does all that she can?" He responded," I like fixing on stuff coach. When I get some money I'm gonna get antique cars and fix them up, inside and out. I know everybody think I'm a mess up and that I won't do nothing with my life, but I am. I'm gonna take care of my grandma cause she the only one who has ever done anything for me."

I went inside the gym to get Zach. We went to my office. Once we entered, he stood as Max remained seated. I stood with my back against the wall just in case Zach decided to hit him. I was going to initiate the conversation, but Michael began to speak." Zach I'm sorry dog. I was just joking, but I should not have done it. I don't have anything against gay people." Zach just stood there like he wanted to beat the crap out of Max. I walked over, stood beside Zach, and said, "Do you accept his apology Zach?" He never took his eyes off Max. If looks could kill, Max would be dead! He said, "Yeah I guess so. They went back into the gym.

A few weeks went by. Friday toward the end of seventh period, Max came running in the gym. It was always intriguing to watch him run because he was slew foot. I dismissed the girls and went to my office. Max followed. I could hear the girls whispering, "What he doing in here with our Coach!" I started straightening my office as usual before going home. Max said, "Coach I just wanted to let you know that me and my grandma talked to the people at Job Corp. They have a mechanic class and I can be certified in two years. They gonna help me get a GED too!" The bell rung as he was talking and he hurried to finish. "I just wanted to tell you that. Thanks Coach! See ya Monday." He took off before I could say anything. I smiled looked toward the ceiling and said, "Thank you Jesus!"

CHAPTER 24

Orlando

Peer pressure can lead to bullying, which in turn can lead to drugs or even to the extreme of carrying a weapon to defend oneself.

I never realized how many students transferred in and out of schools until I started teaching. There were a lot of kids transferring to the school. I had the pleasure of meeting Orlando my first year. He was African-American. He was skinny with a brown paper bag skin complexion. He kept his hair cut short. He wore nice clothes and appeared very quiet. He had a little swag to his walk and on top of that he was bow legged. The girls went crazy and as usual broke their necks to try and get his attention.

I never had him in my class, but he dated one of my basketball girls, Willow. She was a little over average height. She had big eyes that at times seemed as though they were going to pop out of socket. Her skin complexion was dark and boy did she hate that!!! She was bow legged as well. All of the girls held a place in my heart, but she had a special place. She went through a lot mentally and physically. Her mom, Alina and I worked together as a team effortlessly to keep her on the right path.

She reminded me so much of myself. She kept a lot bottled up inside. She was a great kid, very respectable always saying, "Yes ma'am and no ma'am. She made good grades. I used to call Orlando my son-in-law because she was like a daughter to me. He was a good kid as well, but I later learned that he had an anger management problem. He got upset quickly over anything. He was very competitive.

Willow came to me during the middle of their relationship and told me how he began acting different. His jealousy led to anger when it came down to her. He did not want another boy talking to her, looking at her, or walking beside her. WOW!!! I always told the girls they were too young to get involved in serious relationships. I told them they should enjoy being a kid, but what teenager listens! ☺ Willow was a year older than Orlando. Therefore, when she graduated and went to the ninth grade, he was still at the junior high in the eighth grade.

That year early in the school term, around October, Rochelle came to my office one morning. She was on the eighth grade basketball team. She was tall and very skinny. She was African-American. She wore glasses and had a smile that made anyone feel warm inside. She had a very smooth amber brown skin complexion. She had a heart of gold and cared about everybody and everything, just like me. She came from a very good nuclear family who invited me over one Saturday for dinner. It was the first formal house invitation I had. I was very impressed and felt proud to see my *race* showing morals, values, and good Christian beliefs. She was not the best athlete on the team, but that girl could shoot the lights out when she got hot during games. I'm talking long three point shots.

She knocked on the door and came in. She sat down and said, "Coach I think somebody is dealing with a lot and need some help." I said, "Why do you think they need help? Who is it?" She replied, "It's a boy and you really know him. All week on the bus he been getting high?" I said, "Getting high *how?*" She responded, "Smoking weed Coach. I asked him why he been smoking weed and he said he been dealing with a lot of shit. I tried to tell him that smoking was not the answer, but he would not listen. I don't want to get him in trouble Coach, but I also don't want to take the fall if the bus driver find or smell the weed. He sit in the back where I sit. He had a bag of it this morning." I could seriously see the concern in her eyes as she sat there. I said, "Let me see what I can do and as always I never reveal my sources."

Without hesitation I knew I was going to let Mr. Sharpe or Mr. Joyner know. Drugs were a definite no no, but before I could let them know what was going on, I had another visitor. It was Willow. I was always glad when they came back to visit me. ⬚ It told me my "tough love" and my big heart motto paid off. She had a doctor's appointment and stopped to see me before going to school. I thought it was kind of strange for her to visit so early in the morning though.

She came in my office and gave me a big hug. She said, "Ooohhwweee Coach I miss *YOU* so much. It's so different. I mean it's cool being at the high school, but you not up there with us." I asked, "How was everything going? Do you like basketball? How are your teachers?" She answered, "The teachers are alright. My classes are straight. I don't know how I'm gonna do in math. I hate math Coach. All I can say in terms of basketball is that it's not *YOU* coach!"

She paused then continued on, "I came to talk to you about Orlando. Coach he dealing with a lot. I'm worried about him. I keep telling him to come talk to you, but I guess he hasn't. He told me he was. Anyway, he got on the bus with a gun. It's in his book bag. He pulled it out and showed me!" She and Orlando broke up over the summer. I stood up and began slowly pacing the floor because this was a very serious issue. The first thing I asked was, "Why does he have a gun?" She replied, "He say some of the boys picking on him. Talking bout he think he can just come over here and take all the girls. He think he can get their position on the football team, basketball team and track team. They been trying to jump on him I guess. He say he tired and he gonna show them."

I wasted no time trying to go find him like I usually do, but on my way to the counselor's office I slowed down and went to Mr. Sharpe and informed about the situation. Mr. Sharpe was a skinny African-American.

He was the assistant principal. He wore small glasses and kept a low haircut. His hair was salt and pepper as well as his mustache. Every time he talked, that mustache moved in the strangest way. It was kind of curled like the man on the Pringles box. Sometimes I could not help but stare at it.

He knew the students respected and definitely trusted me. One of the main things I like about him was the fact that he practiced Christianity every day. He avoided gossip. His only concern was making sure the students were on the right path. He was a straight forward kind of guy. He definitely took no crap from anyone. Most importantly, he communicated with the students on a daily basis. When students got in trouble, he thoroughly explained the process to them and found a way to give them hope to get on the right path.

After talking to Mr. Sharpe I went back to my office to prepare for my next class. The lesson for that week in PE was softball. I was teaching drills that week. I took my class outside, set up some bases and they engaged in a throwing and running activity. I remember the day well because it was very hot outside and the kids were complaining as usual, but they knew I was not paying the complaining any attention. All of a sudden I felt someone walking up behind me. I turned my head and it was Mr. Joyner.

He was the other assistant principal. He was African-American. He was average height and had gorgeous brown skin. He was young and shy. He used proper pronunciation of his words all the time!!! I later learned he was married to an English teacher at the high school. Maybe that is why he used proper English all the time. ☺ If I stood with my back toward him and heard only his voice, I thought he was Caucasian. His voice had this country southern drawl in it. He was okay. I could tell he was new to the principal thang.

We stood side by side once he made it to where I was standing. We were facing the kids and made no eye contact. The kids were very nosy and always wanted to know what was going on when a principal entered the room. From the look on their faces they thought they were in trouble. I use to want to laugh so bad from their facial expressions, but I maintained my composure. Mr. Joyner began to speak, "I just wanted to personally let you know that we got Orlando. There was in fact a gun in his bag. He is gone. The police came and got him a few minutes ago." I said, "I'm glad you all got to him before he hurt anyone." He turned to walk back to his office, but not before saying, "Good job coach!"

PART III: THE OUTCOME

CHAPTER 25

The Bullying Cycle

The bullying cycle is a repeated form of bullying. Most of the time it happens unexpectedly meaning the bullied is unaware they are now a bully. It is usually the older kids who create patterns of bullying, hazing, or torturing younger kids. One would think the ones who were bullied would put an end to the cycle or at least be a part of the solution instead of the problem. Peer pressure is nine times out of ten the reason for that. The bullying cycle can occur in three different phases: 1) the person being bullied becomes a bully because they want others to feel what they have went through, 2) the person being bullied forms a protective shield which in turn leads them to become a bully or 3) peer pressure leads them to be a bully.

The first phase can occur out of anger as a result of being the victim of bullying. Surprisingly, the bullying cycle took a toll on Bay Bay. I began to see a change in her personality toward the middle of the school term. She even began to give me problems. Bay Bay began to show signs of the first phase toward the middle of her seventh grade year. She was an emotional bully. I had her in my second period PE class and even though she always had respect for me, when she thought I was not watching or around, I noticed how she was very rude to her classmates.

During class instruction, she was very mean to the sixth graders. I had her in my office numerous of times due to that. She possessed exceptional leadership skills, but she began to use those skills as a means to run over her peers. She continued to have respect for me, but I was the only person she had respect for. Her teachers started coming to me because she was being disobedient in class. She was a straight A student. At one point her grades began to fall. She was still making good grades, but they were not A's.

The second phase occurs when a person realize they have had enough of people bullying them and decides to protect themselves by any means necessary. They become very defensive and sometimes physical towards *anyone*. They do not go around looking to bully others, but if by chance someone crosses their path the wrong way, they will most definitely let them know by protecting and defending themselves.

Kennedy began to hang around a "tough" click of girls. They were flunkies and had a bad reputation, but Kennedy felt safe and grew stronger by the day being around them. She was still a quiet good kid, but the look she wore on her face every day after the bullying incident did not show signs of a good kid. She looked as if at any moment she was ready to fight. Her guards were up extremely high, especially toward her peers!!!

One particular day while taking my class to eat in the cafeteria things took a turn for the worse. My class was in line waiting to get their food on the right side. I was standing at the microwave heating up my lunch on the left side of the cafeteria. I always thought that cafeteria was unique.

It had two sections for students to enter and select their food. The cafeteria was attached to the hall which led to classrooms. There was a wall that separated the food from the seating area as well as a door to enter and one to exit after picking up the food.

As I stood waiting on my food my ears and eyes were open just as they were on a day to day basis when I took my class to lunch, I began to notice students getting louder and shifting in their seats. Once my food finished I walked over to the table and sat with my class. I was not even sitting for ten seconds before a fight broke out. There was no teacher supervising that class at the moment. I had no idea where the teacher was, probably walking around somewhere as usual gossiping. I did not know who was fighting, but once I grab one of the girls to separate them, I could not believe who my eyes were seeing. It was Kennedy.

The teachers had already given her a "bad reputation" the year before. Instead of taking the time to get to know her, they decided they did not want to be bothered with her. They were scared of her. Therefore, whenever she got in trouble they wrote her up, sent her to in school isolation (ISI), or made sure she got suspended for a few days. I never had her in any of my classes, but I wish I had. It would have given me a chance to help her more with her problems.

When she realized it was me, she stopped. I calmly told the girls get their book bags and come with me. Stephanie was who she fighting. There was total silence as we walked the hall to the office. It was toward the end of the school year and all of the principal's offices were full of disobedient children. Ms. Cumberland, one of the assistant principals, asked me to take them to her office until she got back. It had a conference room connected to it. I put Stephanie in Ms. Cumberland's office and Kennedy in the conference room.

I talked with Stephanie first to see what started the altercation. Stephanie was African-American. Her skin complexion was very dark, but somewhat smooth. She was much taller and bigger than Kennedy. I did not have her in any of my classes, but I knew her reputation and she was known for telling lies and being messy amongst her peers. As I entered the room to get her side of the story she could not even look at me. She knew exactly who I was and that I did not tolerate anything from anyone.

I stood as she remained seated and I asked, "What's going on? Why were you two fighting?" She said, "I didn't do anything coach. She just attacked me for no reason!" I remained silent after she responded and just stood there with my back against the wall and looked at her. My instincts were telling me she was lying. Honestly, I did not want to hear anymore. From the looks of it, she got the worse end of the fight anyway. Her hair was all over the place. Her clothes were tore and she had a busted lip.

I went in the conference room and sat next to Kennedy. She was still pissed off. Her hands were tapping the desk and she was looking straight ahead. Her legs were shaking and her feet were rocking from side to side. I asked, "Kennedy what happened? Why were you fighting?" Still upset she replied, "Coach she was talking mess and disrespecting my name. She was spreading rumors and lying on me. When I confronted her, she started getting all loud so I hit her in the face."

I placed my hand on hers to calm her down before proceeding to speak. She was still shaking, but once I touched her, she stopped. I told her to look at me. As she looked at me I said, "Kennedy I am disappointed in you. You are an intelligent young lady who should not be acting this way. Why would you let something that someone said make you fight or get under your skin? You're better than that."

The tears began to roll down her face. I was still holding one of her hands. She looked at me and said, "Coach I'm tired of people walking all over me. If I don't stand up for myself who will? They keep thinking I'm weak and won't fight back. I apologize for disappointing you."

I said, "I expect a lot from you. I want you to do something positive with your life. I understand you standing up for yourself and not letting people walk all over you, but you are going to have to learn to control your anger and frustration. People are going to talk about until the day you die. As long as you know the truth about who you are and what you do, that's all that matters. Stand up and face me." We joined hands and I started to pray:

> "Dear Heavenly Father, first and foremost of our lives, thank you for watching over us throughout this day. Father can you please at this very moment lay your hands on Kennedy's heart and spirit. Give her wisdom and strength to trust in you. Be her protector Jesus and let no harm come her way. Help her to forgive those who hurt her emotionally and physically. Bless her to be the bigger and better person during confrontation. In your name, I do pray. Amen."

I opened my eyes and hugged her. She squeezed me very tight. I told her my door was always open if she needs someone to talk to. I opened the door and went back to the cafeteria to my class. I worried about Kennedy a lot the remainder of the week. I prayed for her every night from that point on. She eventually ended up getting suspended for the fight.

The third phase occurs when younger kids want to be just like their older peers. Therefore, they do any and everything to fit in as a result of peer pressure. My last year of teaching, I was introduced to a different type of sixth grade group. The previous years all of the sixth graders were in their classes together, meaning they did not have classes with the seventh and eighth graders. Unfortunately, in PE because the state of Mississippi began to require students take PE to enforce being healthy and physically active, the classes in the gym increased. There were actually four classes the gym at one time. Two of us had sixth grade classes. The other two teachers had seventh and eighth grade classes. It was not long before the seventh and eighth graders began to have a negative impact on the sixth graders.

The fact that the sixth grade group was noticeably a bully group did not make matters any better. I had never seen anything like that before. We had to monitor the boys' locker room as well as the girls' locker room. Every day from the beginning of school until March, there was a bully situation. It got to the point where parents were accusing us because their kids were getting bullied, beat up or picked on. There were some great kids in that particular sixth grade group, but because they were getting bullied, they had to toughen up to defend themselves. That in turn made them bullies to others. I had someone in my office or pulled to the side almost every day. The principals and counselors had them in their office as well trying to solve the problem and reach them in every way possible. Parents were notified and informed as much as possible, but some of them were not willing to cooperate and decided to take matters in their own hands.

One parent in particular, Robert, came to school every day and ate lunch with his son, Dylan. He was mad at us because in his mind we were not doing what we could to protect his son. Dylan was a short and stocky Caucasian boy. He was the spitting image of his dad. He came from a middle class home. From the looks of it, his dad was the only one raising him. As a matter of fact when Mr. Montague came to eat lunch with him, he was on his lunch break from work. He was in my class, but the boy who bullied him was in Ms. Berg's class.

Ms. Berg was African-American. Her skin complexion was like a honey brown. She had a big butt and some curvy hips. She was taller than me. Her waist and stomach was to die for. Every woman wants the waist and stomach she had! She was insecure about her weight and appearance though. I use to always wonder why. I later learned she weighed a lot when she was younger. She got up the strength and motivation to lose the weight prior to teaching at Pearl. She always ate low fat everything from gum to snacks to food. She always had me trying some fat free food. I do not know how she ate it because it was horrible to me. She wore a retainer in her mouth. Her nerves were bad because she did more hollering and yelling at her students than anyone I had ever met. Sometimes I just looked at her and laughed because I was the total opposite, very *PATIENT* when it came to kids. That year was her first year teaching at Pearl and junior high kids. She definitely had more years of teaching experience than I. I was assigned to be her mentor. She and I became very close, something that I rarely did with co-workers, but she earned her trust points with me. I valued her opinion on teaching just as much as she valued mine. We worked together as a team.

Will was tall, skinny, and Caucasian as well. He was very popular amongst his peers. He came from a high income family. They both were very respectable to us, but in the locker room and even during class participation, they were horrible. Will bullied Dylan in the locker room and during class. He took Dylan lunch money. He hid his clothes to make him late for his next class. He talked about how his dad could not afford to buy things other kids had. Ms. Berg and I sat down numerous of times with Will and Dylan to resolve the issue. A month or so went by and everything was okay between the two, but it eventually went back to the bullying.

The PE department had forms the students and parents read and signed at the beginning of every year. The form basically listed the rules for participation in class, consequences for being disobedient, and stated we (teachers) were not liable for any missing items. Those forms came in handy because that is what Ms. Berg and I used to get Mr. Montague and other parents off of our backs. Once they seen their signature on that paper, there was nothing they could do or say.

As we were walking back to the gym from lunch one day, I pulled Will to the side because I wanted to get an understanding of where the bullying was coming from. We began to walk slowly to distance ourselves from the class.

I began, "Will I don't know much about you, but from what I see in class you are a very active person. I know you love PE. How are your grades in your other classes?" Surprisingly, there was no hesitation. He opened up and responded, "My grades okay coach, but I know they could be better. I have B's and C's. I can't stand math or reading." I asked, "Who do you live with? Who raise you?" He said, "I live with my aunt. She has raised me since birth. My mom did not want me when I was born so my aunt took me. She has two kids of her own."

At that exact moment my heart fell. I just wanted to grab and hug him, but I had to remain tough until I got to the root of the bullying. I said, "I am going to ask you something and I want you to be honest with me. This conversation is between you and me. Tell me why you are so mean to Dylan? Has he done something to you?"

By then we were approaching the gym and he paused for a moment. I mean he stood dead still in his tracks. By the time I realized he had stopped I was a few feet in front of him. I stopped as well. He dropped his head and was staring at the concrete. He slowly responded, "Coach I am not a mean person, but my life has not been easy like everyone else's. I come to school and listen to everybody talk about things they do with their mom and dad and I don't have anything to say because my mom left me. I don't know who my dad is. I just want to belong. I want to feel important that's all."

I said, "Do you be mean to Dylan cause others tell you to then?" He said, "I see everybody else doing it so I do it coach. They notice me when I be mean to Dylan. I get respect and everything."

We sat on the steps outside the gym. I looked at him and said, "Does any of what you just told me make any sense? Do you think it's right? How would you feel if someone did that to you?" What he said next blew me away. He said, "Coach I have had someone bully me. My aunt's two kids have picked on me since I was eight. They do not do it anymore cause I stand up for myself now." I asked, "Does anyone pick on you at school?" He answered, "No ma'am, but I look up to older boys especially the ones who play soccer cause I want to play bad. When I see some the guys pick on Dylan in the locker room, I join in."

He had his head dropped as we continued sitting on the steps. His body language showed regret. I was comfortably leaning back on the top step staring out at the landscaping. I leaned forward and said, "Will I want you do something for me." He said, "What's that coach?" I said, "I want you to believe in yourself and stop depending on others to be successful in life. You know in your heart what's right and what's wrong so do what's right. I know what it's like to want to fit in and be a part of a group at your age, but as you get older and get out into the real world, you are going to see that not belonging to a group will be better for you. Stop being mean to Dylan. If you don't have nothing nice to say to him, don't say nothing at all. Do you think you can try and do what I am asking you to?"

He looked at me with those big brown eyes and replied, "I think I can do that coach. At least I am gonna try." I smiled and said, "My door is always open if you need to talk about anything. Now go get dressed."

One day as the classes were getting dressed to engage in the activity for the day, I noticed a lot of mini groups standing in circles gossiping. After checking roll, Ms. Berg walked over to me and said, "Coach you are not gonna believe this. The kids in my class said that Mr. Montague went to Will's house to speak with his family about the bullying. Things must have gotten out of hand because Will and Dylan ended up fighting in front of the parents. Mr. Montague was boosting them up and everything." I could not believe what I was hearing.

"That would explain the black eye Dylan has," I responded. We both looked at Will and noticed he had bruises and marks on his face as well. Believe it or not after that day we had no more problems in terms of Will bullying Dylan. I thought, "Was that the right thing for Mr. Montague to do? Whatever happened to kill em with kindness? Maybe sometimes fighting back will keep a victim from being bullied."

CHAPTER 26

Suicide

Children who are bullied are nine times more likely to attempt suicide.

Suicide crossed my mind almost every day, from the time I got on the bus to go to school until I got home. I talked to Jesus a lot every bus ride home. I slept in the mornings or either studied for a test or did homework. I believed in utilizing what little time I had to myself wisely. Depression was heavy during those years. I hoped a car ran me over as I crossed the street and killed me. When the school took us on field trips to the zoo, I felt like jumping inside the tigers' cage as their food for the day. Whenever I had to take some medicine I wanted to take as much as I could, overdose, and die. The only problem with overdosing was if someone found me in time, I would get rushed to the hospital. The doctors would pump my stomach and save me. Then I would have to explain why I wanted to die.

I wrote a letter to Mrs. Bright my eighth grade year. I just did not know what else to do. I was depressed. Nothing was working for me. I continued to pray because that was the only thing that I had to keep me mentally sane, but even praying was beginning to feel like a waste of time. I was mad at Jesus because I read the bible and applied it to my life every day in every way, but it was not working. The letter was simple and straight to the point. I sealed it up in a regular envelop. I gave it to Ardeshia and told her to give it to Mrs. Bright. It was written in green ink and it read,
"*Dear Mrs. Bright,*

> *I miss you so much. Things are different up here. I hate my life. The kids are mean to me. I suck in basketball. No one wants to be my friend. I am going to commit SUICIDE soon!!! I just don't want to live anymore. Please don't tell my family.*
>
> *Laketta*"

A few days went by and I was beginning to worry because I had not heard from her. It was early in the morning and I was in Ms. Bowman's Pre-Algebra class. I was zoned out that day and just going through the motions. Actually, I was thinking of ways to kill myself.

I thought about going to the bathroom and throwing myself into the mirrors that were on the wall. Once I broke the mirrors, I was going to take a piece of the glass and cut my wrist. If that did not work I was going to stab myself in the stomach and bleed to death on the floor. I thought about getting a pencil and stabbing myself in the eye. The football field was close to the highway. During basketball practice, Coach Johnson had us run a mile around the field sometimes. I thought of a plan to cut between the trees, run into the highway, and get hit by an eighteen wheeler and die on the spot. There were many suicidal ideas running through my mind.

Then all of a sudden, there was a knock at the door. My thoughts were interrupted. It was one of the counselor aids. She walked up to the teacher and then over to me. She knelt down beside my desk and quietly said, "The counselor needs to see you in her office. Come with me." I packed my book bag and followed her to the office. As good as my memory is, I honestly have no clue what the counselor's name was.

I walked in and just stood there until I was instructed to do otherwise. The counselor, Ms. Jennings, was sitting at her desk. Her office was very cluttered. She was Caucasian and young. She was a brunette. Her body size was average. She had a thin waist and was a few inches taller than me. She said, "Have a seat Laketta." I slowly sat down. I had never been in the counselor's office before. Truthfully, I never went to the office period unless it was to get an excuse for being absent. The principal's office and the counselor's office were all in the same building.

Once I sat down, it was silent for a few minutes. I was staring at the front of her desk toward the floor. Then she said, "Laketta how are? How have things been going for you?" I responded, "I'm okay. Things been okay?" As I was responding, I noticed she had leaned forward. Her hands were clenched together under her chin. She did not take her eyes off of me. She continued, "I pulled your grades and they are exceptional. I noticed you are in a few organizations as well. I received a letter from Mrs. Bright today. She asked me to talk to you." At that very moment I could feel the rage growing inside of me. I was mad at Mrs. Bright for telling the counselor about my letter. I wanted *her* to help me, not some stupid counselor.

I showed no signs of my rage as I sat there. I shook everything off as quickly as possible in terms of my mood. I looked at the counselor and said, "I'm okay. I just needed someone to talk to. I feel much better now." The counselor knew I was lying. She did her job the best way she knew how and said, "Well Laketta if there is anything I can do for you please come let me know. That's what I am here for."

I gathered my things and went to my next class. For the remainder of the day all I could think was, "Why did Mrs. Bright tell? I trusted her and she betrayed me. I will never talk to her again."

My sophomore year in high school I actually attempted to take my life. I was cleaning up the house one night as usual before going to bed and I came across a bottle of pills. They were prescribed for my momma. After I finished cleaning and making sure my siblings were prepared for the next day, I got a cup from the kitchen and went to the bathroom.

The bathroom was my sanctuary. It was the only place I had peace and time to myself to just breathe. I took the bottle of pills and the cup with me. I filled the cup up with water from the sink. I looked in the mirror and softly said, "I am tired Jesus. I have enough going on here, but the way they treat me at school is unbearable. I don't understand why *you* let them do that to me. I am the nicest person in the world and I still get treated like crap! I guess I will never get to see your face because people who commit suicide go to hell."

I poured a handful of the pills into my hand. I filled the cup with water and drank some. I tilted my head back and slowly dropped the pills in my mouth. The bottle was full. By the time I finished, there was only a few in the bottle. I used the bathroom and went to bed. Ardeshia and I shared a room until we moved out. I laid down beside her on my back and stared at the ceiling until I could not keep my eyelids open anymore. All I knew was that I wanted to die peacefully.

The sun peaked through the window and touched my eyes. I thought, "Damn it didn't work!" I felt horrible from all those pills. As I stood up, my legs felt like they weighed a ton. My head was leaning toward the side. My walk was all off balance as I went to the bathroom. I quickly straightened myself up because I did not want my family to suspect anything.

CHAPTER 27

Counseling

Most people feel uncomfortable when counseling or therapy is recommended. African-Americans will not even consider it. We believe in the power of PRAYER. As it turns out, counseling is not so bad after all. I never told a soul about being bullied until I became a teacher. Then my life took a turn for the worst. I became a teacher in 2007 and lost my job in 2010. (That is a completely different book) Just when I thought all the pain I went through the previous 20 years was finally over, some more came. When it rains it pours. I was finally beginning to see the sun peeking from behind the clouds.

Then all of a sudden it got dark and the rain began to fall! I was depressed, suicidal, and did not want to be bothered. I was mad at God more than anything. I could not believe I went through all those years of hell, got a teaching job, which was my sunshine, and only teach for *THREE* years to lose my job. I kept the faith all of those years and stayed focused on what I believed in no matter what card I was dealt and look at what happened.

My one and only "true friend" Janae Knocks did what real friends are supposed to. Janae is African-American with a smooth brown skin complexion. She is taller than me of course. She loves her tattoos. She is a very strong, independent woman who has no problem speaking her mind! Sometimes that can be an advantage or a disadvantage. She is the true definition of what a "best friend" should be. We have been friends ever since 2004. She was there for me when I lost my job. She suggested therapy and for the first time I actually thought about it.

I did not know where to begin looking for affordable counseling. An old co-worker, Athena, gave me a hotline crisis number. (Pay close attention to how God works!) I called the number and come to find out it was for teenagers. The woman was still genuinely concerned for me and my well-being. She asked, "Do I need to send someone to your home right now?" I was so out of it, but I managed to say, "No." She asked, "Well if I find a counseling center close to you, will you call and set up an appointment?" I said, "Yeah why not." She gave me the address and phone number to a Family Counseling Center five miles from my house.

I hesitated for days about calling. I just did not feel like there was anything that could be done. I was at my lowest low and the last thing I felt like doing was opening up to discuss what I was dealing with. I eventually called to schedule an appointment. Those therapy sessions turned out to be the best thing for me. It was a "Christian" center for marriage and family counseling. The name of it was Theological and Reform Institution. I had two counselors, Lisa and Cindy. They were six or seven years younger than me.

Cindy was tall and Caucasian. She had long blonde hair. Her body size was average. She had a small waist and flat stomach. She was quiet and reserved. She asked me very difficult questions at times throughout my sessions. It was not hard to see that she was a very strong woman who loved God. They did not impose their own personal thoughts on me, but due to my innate ability to observe people, I learned that she and I had a lot in common. We both take our careers very serious. We wear our hearts on our sleeves. We go above and beyond for others while making less time for ourselves.

Lisa on the other hand was very different. She was average height for a woman. She was Caucasian as well with shoulder length hair. It was blonde with brownish streaks in it. She was skinny. She had a wild personality, but kept it under control. She was definitely outspoken when needed. She had a nose ring and a tattoo just as me. She traveled a lot. She and I had a lot in common as well. She also had a heart of gold. She went above and beyond for others, but she knew when to say no and take time for *herself*. I admired her for that.

The root of all my problems went back to the bullying I dealt with as a child as well all the other things I had to take on at an early age. From the first session, they realized that I had many layers and it was going to take some time to peel them back. Cindy looked at me and asked, "Are you willing to continue counseling until we discover all the layers?" I was slouched in my chair staring at the floor, but some kind of way I managed to say, "Yeah…. Sure….Okay….." The institution charged patients based on their income. I only paid TEN dollars every time I had a session, which was once a week. I remember thinking to myself, "If I had known therapy was going to be as successful as it was, I would have went a long time ago.

It is extremely important to introduce counseling to children who are bullied and the children doing the bullying. I am a living witness of the long-term effects it can have on a person's life. I still have nightmares to the very day about how I was treated. It has affected every area of my life. It is hard for me to have any type of relationship because I keep my guard up. I am too scared to let anyone in. I have a hard time trusting people. I am not as close to my family as I would like to be. Isolation has become a way of life for me that I do not even realize when I am doing it. Counseling truly helps. It will not allow a person to go back in time and change what happened, but it will help that person move forward with life in a positive way. One cannot discover their future until they have faced their past.

CHAPTER 28

The Effects of My Bullying

Bullying can have long-term effects on a person. What happens during childhood can set the tone for the rest of one's life, and it is important that it is dealt with early on.

When I look back on my life and the things that I have been through it is painful. There are more dark and rainy days than light and sunny days or at least it feels that way. There were some parts of this book that were exciting to write. My hand could not move as fast as my mind was remembering all the thoughts. Then there were parts of this book that I had to write a little a day on because remembering was painful. There were literally tears on the pages as I wrote.

The older I became, the more I began to evaluate myself on every level as it pertains to the wellness cycle. The wellness cycle basically states that if a person can balance out intellectual, spiritual, physical, mental, emotional, or social attributes then they are healthy. Over the years I have come to learn that on a scale from one to ten, one being the worse and ten being the best that intellectually I am a ten! I am very smart in many ways. A lot of people who are book smart do not have much common sense. The term "dumb blonde" or "air head" is used in reference to them. Then there are people with common sense and no book sense. There is one more type of sense that people overlook and it is "street sense."

Street sense refers more to the hood, street life, or everyday life outside of the professional environment. It is when a person can survive the in *real world* and handle situations as they present themselves by any means necessary. A hustler fits into this category. An "illegal hustler" is a drug dealer, car theft, and other things like that.

A person who survives by any means necessary, but in a good way is a "legal hustler." A single-parent raising kids, working multiple jobs, keeping the house clean and attending their kid's activities is a hustler. A college student is a hustler because they pay tuition, pay for vehicles, books, and maintain good grades throughout the entire process. A teacher is a hustler because in order to be a great teacher, one has to purchase a lot of things. Most of the time they have to pay for it themselves. A coach is a hustler because in order to have a great season one must practice, practice, practice. Coaches have to pick athletes up and take them home. Coaches spend a lot of money out of their pockets for their team. Coaches take the time to have conferences with teachers to ensure good grades. Coaches make house calls and visits with parents to keep their athletes on the right track. True, dedicated coaches never sleep! I have been blessed with all three: book sense, common sense, and street sense.

I take pride in educating myself as much as possible on any and everything. I enjoy reading and writing. I listen to teachers, professors, and people who are older than me or even younger than me for that matter, to gain knowledge, wisdom and understanding. I am always striving to improve my mind. I set goals, whether they are short-term or long-term for myself on a daily basis. I write them down and put them on my refrigerator, wall, calendar, or wherever as long as I can see them every day. Every day that Jesus allows me to wake up I look at the goals and see what I need to do reach them.

I hope to earn a Ph. D in Psychology someday. I want to inspire, motivate, and change lives more than anything. Believe it or not I always end up meeting people who want to talk to me about things they are dealing with in their lives. I have always been told that I have a lot of wisdom for my age, even now that I am thirty. I remember being 20 and giving advice to people who were ten years older than me. That has always been scary because I always think to myself, "Jesus how in the world can I tell them what to do when I am half their age. They will not listen to me." Actually, they did and still do. I multi-task a lot, which can be a downfall at times. I have a tendency to put more on my plate than I can eat, but I eventually consume it all one day at a time.

Spiritually I am a ten. I am a genuine good person. My number one thing is *believing* and keeping the *faith*. I always believe in the unseen. Growing up as a child I always wanted to save all the families in poverty. I always told Jesus if he blessed me with a lot of money, I would give some to those who really need it.

I am a Pisces and we have innate abilities that can be very scary. I see things before they happen. I am not a psychic or anything like that, but I have a very deep intuitive side. Everything that I do has to have a purpose and a meaning. I do not do stuff just to do it. I pay a lot of attention to zodiac signs when I meet people. I can pretty much tell what kind of personality one has based on their zodiac sign. I try to stay away from Gemini's and Sagittarius's. Gemini's have a hard time telling the truth, balancing money, and love talking on the phone so much to the point that they miss on spending quality time with their family. Sagittarius speak their mind a little too much. They do not think before they speak and can come off as saying hurtful things. Of course me having the life that I have, I meet Gemini and Sagittarius all the time. Sometimes I think Jesus put me around those signs to help me stop being so sensitive. Maybe he puts me around them to help them get better with themselves.

I attend church. I do not go every Sunday, but I go at least twice a month. When I go I LISTEN. I stand as the pastor read the scripture that he is going to preach on. I write the scripture down in my small notebook, highlight it in my bible, and write down the topic the pastor preaches on it. I have two versions of the bible to help me understand it more. One is purple, which is the International Version my Aunt San gave to me for Christmas in 2003. The other one is burgundy, which is the original King James Version. I am not perfect by a long shot, but I aim to get as close to perfection as I possibly can. I keep Jesus Christ the head of my life and as hard as it is sometimes, I trust him to guide me in the right direction and stay on the right path in life.

Physically I give myself a five. Of course, people tell me I look nice, especially for my age. ☺ I do not see it that way. My workout regime is INTENSE. It always has been for as long as I can remember. Currently I lift weights four days a week. Two days out of the week I do stomach and leg muscles. Two days a week I do arm and back muscles. I lift weights for toning purposes. The expression and stares I get from people as I work out, especially men, is hilarious, but motivating. I have my mp3 player in my ear. I have to listen to music when I work out because it takes my mind off of what I am doing and it keeps me relaxed. I jog at least two days a week anywhere from two to three miles at a park or through the neighborhood. I love the outdoors. I jog to the beat of the music from my mp3 player.

I love all types of music. I mostly jog to Lil Wayne, T. I., Rhianna, Do or Die, Eminen, Pastor Troy, Nicki Minaj, Ying Yang Twins, Chris Brown, Bone Thugs and Harmony, Three Six Mofia, 50 Cent, Beyonce`, Rick Ross, Adelle, Trey Songs, Brittany Spears, Kirk Franklin, Shirley Ceasar, Mary Mary, Yolanda Adams, Donnie McKirkland, Pattie LaBelle, Whitney Houston, Peabo Bryson, Michael Bolton, Al Green, and many more. Whatever song has an upbeat tempo, I run to it. As long as it is motivational, I work out to it. T.I. song "Motivation" is without a doubt my favorite song to listen to as I jog. Not only does it have a good upbeat tempo for exercising, but the words win me over every time. I can feel what he is saying. Actually, the music I listen to has to have good strong lyrics to catch my attention.

I attend three aerobics classes a week as well. One is called Zumba. It is a mixture of fitness and dance. I have always loved dancing. I feel as if I am at the club getting my groove on. I love it!!! One class is called Spin. I enjoy it as well to the point where I may get certified and become an instructor. We listen to music and ride a stationary bike for forty-five minutes. We ride to the beat of the music and trust me when I say not everyone has rhythm or good coordination. ☺ The last class is called circuit training. It is by far my favorite class to attend. I set my entire schedule around it just to make sure I get to that class. I go twice a week. That is how much I love it!

There are many reasons why I work out so much, but the main reason is to relieve stress. Deep down inside I also work out to make myself feel better from all of the verbal and emotional bullying I went through growing up. It took me a long time to feel comfortable wearing certain clothes. I just started wearing jeans. Every time I put clothes on I look in the mirror to see how my butt, love handles, and stomach look. If I am not comfortable with how those three look I do not wear the outfit. Every time I look at my butt I hear all the things Leon and other boys use to say when I was in school. My skin condition has cleared up remarkably thanks to Palmer's Cocoa Butter Lotion, Tone soap, and Ambi skin cream! I love wearing shorts, especially the really short ones. ☺ I most definitely cherish my three inch heels. I look good in them too.

My confidence level and self-esteem in terms of my body has definitely gotten better. Even though I still have all of those memories in my mind from being called "ugly" all the time, a sista can look in the mirror now and say, "Damn I *do* look good." When people tell me I do not look my age I feel good inside. That tells me that I have been doing something right. I guess one can say my haters were my motivators. ☺ I know I have made a transformation when I go back to my hometown and run into my old classmates. They look at me in astonishment and say, "Ketta you look good girl!"

When the guys who told me I was ugly or never paid me any attention see me and actually have the nerve to try and get my number to take me out on a date, I cannot believe it. They really do not remember being mean to me! I am not one to throw things up in people's face or say I told you so, but my body language and facial expressions say it all as I walk away ignoring them. I politely say, "I'm not interested because I'm too focused on college and my career. I do not have time for a relationship." The next line is, "Well let me give you my number." I say, "You can, but I'm not gonna call you." Then they say, "Damn, why you got to be so mean?" I say, I'm not mean. I just know what I want and I refuse to settle."

Inside I am ecstatic and cannot believe that whoever it was tried to holla at me. The funny thing is all of the guys I have run into since high school that use to be fine to me, look horrible. They have let themselves go. The use to be athletes have beer bellies and are overweight. The girls who did not want to be my friend in school all of a sudden want to chill out with me now. They request to be my friend on Facebook all the time. I do not accept them of course. "Everything you do comes back on you tenfold." You reap what you sow."

Mentally I give myself a three. My mind stays all over the place. My mood and personality change a hundred times a day. Everything affects me. I do not know how to not let stuff bother me so much. I am a worrier. I am a very sensitive person, but no one really knows that unless I actually let them in. I am only tough because I *HAVE* to be not because I *WANT* to be. A lot of people do not understand that concept.

Throughout the years I have created this protective armor to keep those who mean me no good away from me. I have come to realize that I do not let anyone in. I do not trust anyone in anyway. I always have my guards up. If it is something that has to be done in terms of a task whether it is at my job or home, I do it because I feel like if I do not do it, it will not get done right. I do not like that about myself! I keep myself isolated from everyone, which is why I do not have friends. I feel like everyone is out to destroy me or bring me down. I do not hang around too many women at all. I do socialize, but to a minimum. I do not know if I am that way because I grew up with no friends and it became a way of life or if that is just the way it is. The strange thing is I want friends, but I am too scared to let them inside my world. It is like I want it, but I don't.

Sometimes I think I am bipolar because of my moods. I get heavily depressed at times. Then all of a sudden I am happy. When I am down, I'm down and there is usually nothing no one can do to cheer me up. I have to come out of it myself in my own way, which is mostly through prayer. The good thing is when I am happy, I am happy. No one really knows that about me because I cover things up so well. When I took counseling I asked if they thought I was crazy or something was wrong with me mentally. They did not think so. Cindy said, "No one person is the same every day. There are all kinds of things that trigger different moods and emotions in people all the time." They informed me before I had my first session that if they felt the need to refer me to a mental institution or doctor, they would with my permission. I was cool with that.

Sometimes I feel like I do not even know who I am. I have spent my entire life being supportive of and doing for everybody that I have not had time to *find* or shall I say *show* who I really am. (That's another book in the making.) I have always had to be the strong one, the "rock." When the "rock" shows weakness or cry, everything around them falls as well.

I can count on one hand how many serious personal relationships I have been in. I want to be in love and be happy, but I do not know how to let someone in. Maybe I do know how, but just too scared to. I am afraid they will not accept me for who I am or be able to deal with me. I can be a lot to deal with at times. I have no problem on the other hand accepting a person for who they are. When I love, I love hard and unconditionally. It is all or nothing with me. I have a giving heart and soul. I am a protector. The problem is I do not know how to *receive*.

I am not taking any crap from anybody in a relationship. Absolutely no kind of abuse and no cheating. If cheating occurs and I find out, which I always do because everything done in the dark comes to light, I quietly leave. I do not say anything or ask why. I am a hopeless romantic who believes as long as there is love one can get through anything, but RESPECT and LOYALTY goes a longer way than love. I do know what it means to go through the ups and downs in a relationship. It takes hard work and dedication to make a relationship last. Every day is not going to be a good day. Communication is key and without it problems will occur daily whether they focus on finances, cheating, children, in-laws, and many other issues.

Emotionally I give myself a four. I am very sensitive. I wear my heart on my sleeves. I cry easily and it depends on who I am around as far as letting them see me cry. There is one important lesson for people who wear their heart on their sleeves and that is knowing who to let see it and who not to. Of all the life-long lesson I have had to learn, that one has by far been the hardest one to learn. I learned that lesson in 2010 and it hurt like hell too because of what I had to go through to learn it. It is not good to let everybody see your heart. As a kid growing up I did not cry in front of people because I was embarrassed and ashamed or because I was the "rock." Being the rock means not letting people see you cry or know you are hurting inside or so I thought.

Now if I do not let anyone see me cry it is because it shows weakness and even though I understand that I cannot be strong all the time and it is okay to cry, it still takes a lot to allow someone to see me cry. I cry a lot when I am alone. I have good crying and bad crying. Bad crying is when I am in pain or hurting because of something or somebody. Bad crying is when I am stressed out about my career, college, or especially when my money is not right.

Good crying is when I watched my girls win a basketball game or accomplish a certain skill because I taught them and they actually listened. Good crying is when I watch an inspirational movie whether it is *Bambi, Cinderella, Remember the Titans, Gridiron Gang, The Color Purple,* or any love story as well as those athletic movies based on true stories. Good crying is when I see kids helping other kids. Good crying is I look at how my mom has turned her life around and is being a *mother* now. Good crying is when I see how strong my little sisters, Biancca and Davina are. When I realize that I do not have to worry about them getting the opportunity to go to college and being productive citizens I cry tears of joy. Good crying is when I see they do not have to go through as much as I did when I was their age. They actually get to see what is like to be a CHILD and have FUN!!!

My feelings get hurt easily. I am like a Champaign flute that shatters at the high pitches of an opera singer's voice. I am fragile. I hurt a lot because people do not know me. Why? Is it because I have isolated myself so much due to bullying and other personal experiences which causes me to not let anyone inside my world? Who knows? What is done, is done. Regardless of what the reason is, I have to fix that. It is going to take a while too. It is very hard, but I have been putting my best foot forward. I am very impatient. I want stuff my way. I want what I want when I want it!

Socially, it is hard to say. I give myself a seven. I keep to myself. I do not too much believe in bothering people. I do what I have to and call it a day. I keep a lot of things I do to myself. I am a good observer, which means I watch people and learn how they are very quick. It is so surprising because I observe and notice things without even trying to. Once I get a feel on what kind of person someone is, it determines how I react with them. I can usually tell within ten minutes whether or not a person is someone I want in my life.

I get referred to as "antisocial" sometimes because I am usually quiet when I first meet someone or if I have been around someone for a while and does not engage in conversation with them, which is usually because they are not someone I want to be around because of their ways or personality!!! Overall once a person gets to know me, I am someone they want to keep in their lives. Don't get me wrong when I am out and about in the world, I am a nice person. I was raised to speak and say, "have a nice day" growing up, but I sometimes go no further than that. As I stated before, I meet all kind of people who do not even know me when I am out in society who just walk up to me and talk about things they are going through in life. As usual I do the best that I can to just listen and give the best advice.

Honestly, I do not open up to well to people. I wear a very strong protective shield and if at any moment I allow someone inside my world they are considered "blessed" because I do not do that too often. I believe I mainly do that because once a person sees the real me, it may be too much for them and they may not know how to deal with it. I can be a bit much at times. I am a very organized, precise, loyal, and honest person who expects the same. If by chance I do not receive what I give out, the consequences can be surprising.

CHAPTER 29

The Solution to Bullying

Bullying laws were created to prevent bullying and address it when it happens. They are also known as "anti-bullying laws." They focus on schools, middle schools (6-8), where of a lot bullying occurs. There are forty-five states that enforce and recognize the bullying laws. The laws focus on training public school staffs in addressing bullying, intimidation, harassment, and suicide prevention. WOW! THAT'S GREAT! The question now is do the schools utilize these laws?

The American Academy of Child and Adolescent Psychiatry estimates that half of all children are bullied at some point during their school years. Almost 10% of children are bullied repeatedly.

There will probably never be a solution to end bullying, but it can be decreased. If people work together to "understand" bullying, then it will be easier to create methods and strategies, which in turn will lead to interventions. The key word is "understand" and analyze. Bullying has to be studied thoroughly. It is more to it than knowing what to do and say when someone is a victim of bullying. Actually, the bully is the one who needs to be analyzed and helped more than anything.

Most children and adolescents bully others for three reasons: 1) they have low self-esteem therefore they bully others to make themselves feel good 2) they were bullied themselves as a result of the bullying cycle and 3) peer pressure. When studying children from ages six to eleven most of them bully because of peer pressure. They see their peers picking on others and they do it to fit in. They fail to realize that they are hurting, whether it is physically or emotionally, others. Adolescents bully to make themselves feel better or above others. Some are results of the bullying cycle. What is surprising is most bullies come from good homes. They are a part of a nuclear family. Some are raised in good single-parent homes also. Either way they are raised with morals and high expectations. Religion is enforced in the homes as well.

During my teaching career, it tore my heart to pieces when a parent(s) said, "Coach I don't know what's going on. I DID NOT RAISE MY CHILD THAT WAY!" As a teacher, we see sides of children that parents never believe. We actually see children more hours of the day than most parents. Children are in school eight hours a day. Some children go home to an empty house because their parent(s) have not made it home from work. Some go home and go to their room to get on the internet, play video games, or talk on their cell phone. Others do not have that close relationship with their parents and do not care to be at home. Therefore, they go outside and play or go to a neighbor's house.

Parent(s) have to cook, clean, do laundry, pick children up from after school practices from involvement in extracurricular activities among many other things. All of these things plus many more keep parents from being around their children and seeing who they really are. There are some parents who know exactly who their children are and how they treat others, but even angels fall sometimes. No one is perfect. As a teacher we see ALL of those sides on a day to day basis.

Listed below are some important guidelines to assist teachers, administrators, and parents with bullying issues.

WHAT ARE THE SIGNS OF SOMEONE BEING BULLIED?

1. Low self-esteem
2. Quiet
3. Keep to themselves
4. First one to class or last one to leave class
5. Sit close to teacher's desk or front of class
6. Cling to teacher who's on duty
7. Act out in class
8. Weight problem (obese or underweight)
9. Get into fights with same person repeatedly
10. Disability impairment
11. Compare themselves to others
12. Do not feel pretty/handsome
13. Talk about death/suicide regularly
14. Anti-social
15. Play "hookie"
16. Don't want to go to school
17. Unexplained bruises or injuries
18. Come home without clothes or items
19. Do not participate in activities or class especially PE
20. Talk about protecting themselves a lot

WHAT ARE THE SIGNS OF A BULLY?

1. Loud and outspoken
2. Bad attitude
3. Stay in trouble
4. Hang around unusual crowds to make themselves feel superior or better about themselves
5. Come from broken home
6. Use size and height to own advantage

7. Good child
8. Make good grades
9. Hang around bad crowd who influences them to bully
10. Want to fit in or belong
11. Peer pressure
12. Afraid they will get bullied if they don't bully

WHAT TO DO IF YOU ARE A TEACHER:

1. Be compassionate
2. Pay attention at all times!!! Observe!
3. Push and pull equilibrium: If a child comes to you because he/ she is being bullied, take your time and LISTEN. You do not want to show too much concern because the child will cling to you. You do not want to show too little concern because the child will think you do not care.
4. Talk to the school counselor to get background information on child; create an intervention that includes the child, counselor, and parent
5. Get permission from child and/or parent(s) to address the issue with the bully; even if child says no find a way to get them to understand that you need to talk with the parent and/or bully
6. Find a connection, a way to let child know you understand what they are going through; tell some personal experience or obstacle that you have overcome
7. Be patient and wise; children who are bullied are very gentle
8. Be trustworthy and loyal; let the child know they can trust you and anything that you do is for their benefit.
9. Follow-up; keep checking on the child throughout the year to see how things are going; not every day though

WHAT TO DO IF YOU ARE A PARENT OF A BULLIED CHILD:

1. Talk and COMMUNICATE with your child!!!
2. Assure the child that you will be there no matter what
3. PRAY, PRAY, PRAY
4. Set up conferences with the principal, teacher, parent of the bully, and their child
5. Do not encourage the child to initiate a fight with the bully. Instead teach the child defense mechanisms such as karate, boxing, etc., in case the bully attacks them

6. Explain to the child how important it is to stand up for themselves rather it is vocally or physically. (Sometimes a victim may get beat up, but that bully will know that the child has heart and will put up a fight to prove a point; which is they will no longer be bullied)
7. Be available at all times, as much as possible
8. Pay attention to your child's mood or personality change

WHAT TO DO IF YOU ARE BEING BULLIED:

1. Tell someone preferably an adult: parent, teacher, or principal
2. Never be alone around the bully, be with a group
3. Calmly tell bully to leave you alone and walk away or write a letter; AVOID VIOLENCE
4. Be active in school events and stay around positive people
5. Ignore text messages or emails; make a copy and show to an adult

CHAPTER 30

The Bullying Challenge

The bullying challenge is for people who are willing to step up no matter what and do the right thing to prevent bullying. When someone steps up to the bullying challenge, they are willing to:

1. Stand up and tell a bully to stop
2. Defend a victim
3. Tell an authority figure that someone is getting bullied
4. Do all they can to raise bullying awareness
5. SPEAK OUT AND SPEAK UP

If you are an athlete, you have received that gift for a reason. Your peers look up to you, your coach expects you to be a leader and set a good example, and your parents want you to always do the right thing and be respectful. Do not be afraid to speak up if you see someone doing wrong because nine times out of ten, they will listen. There are more people who look up to you than you think. You are natural born leaders whether you want to be or not. Are you ready for the bullying challenge?

If you are a teacher, you are most definitely in a position to inspire and save lives. Sadly, there are some of you who could care less about the children you teach. All you care about is a paycheck and your reputation. Children are smarter than you think. They know what teachers are truly there for them. Observe, listen, and show concern for your students. Will you recognize a bully and pull them to side to be a part of the bullying challenge?

If you are counselor, do not just sit in your office on the computer all day rearranging classes and putting children in PE, Art, or Band because their Math teacher cannot deal with them anymore. Stand outside your office and walk the halls during class change. Jesus gave you the gift of listening, advising, and seeing a child's heart and soul. Can you accept the bullying challenge?

If you are a parent, you have the hardest responsibility in the world. Raising children is a full time job. Good parents never get a break. They work twenty-four hours a day, seven days a week. It is your job to protect and pay attention to your children as much as possible. Your children look up to you more than they do anyone else. They expect you to protect them. Most children do not even notify their parent(s) when they are getting bullied. It is your responsibility to sense it and ask questions. If your child is getting bullied and do come to you, go above and beyond until the problem is solved.

You may be the parent who was a BULLY in school. Maybe you knew it, maybe you did not. The fact of the matter is "everything you do comes back on you ten times worse than what you done to someone else!" Ask for forgiveness, take a deep breath, and be there for your child the best way possible. Assure your child that trouble does not last always! Weeping may endure in the night, but joy comes in the morning! You cannot get mad, go to the school or neighborhood and fight the parent or bully. I know you may want to because that is a parent's natural instinct to protect their child by any means necessary. Instead, be a responsible, logical, respectable adult. Remember your child is "watching" you more than you think. Your actions dictate the way they will be as they get older. Please make sure and handle the situation by remaining calm and taking all the necessary steps. Will you become a part of the bullying challenge?

CHAPTER 31

My Cup Runneth Over

Let us not become weary in doing good, for at the proper time we will reap a harvest if we do not give up. (Galatians 6:9 NIV)

I was reminded daily how Jesus did not forget about me. I received more blessings than I could handle, but there were two days I will never forget: my birthday and the seventh grade field trip. Birthdays mean a lot to me and for many reasons, but the main reason is because it is a special day Jesus has made just for "you." Important people should not forget one's birthday. It is not about the gifts, but instead the sentimental meaning behind the occasion. Just hearing someone say "happy birthday" on the actual day is the best feeling in the world.

My basketball girls and even my students knew how I felt about birthdays. My birthday fell toward the end of basketball season. It was my first year teaching and coaching. The eighth grade girls worked hard during the off season that year. The results up until February were a perfect 8-0. We lost to our rivalry three days before my birthday, which was my first lost as a coach. I am very competitive and cannot stand losing. I was heartbroken. I felt as if I had let the girls down. I remember calling my momma for the first time during my own pain and just crying. Surprisingly, she said what any mother would have said, "Ketta you can't beat yourself up. Those girls love you and they know it's not your fault. You not gonna win them all baby." Even though I understood what momma said and even felt comforted, I was still mad and disappointed.

My birthday was the same week we lost our first game, but on the weekend. We played two games a week on Tuesday and Thursday. We lost on that Thursday. Friday has always been my favorite day of the week. I felt okay as I taught throughout the day. My co-workers knew the girls respected me and that I did everything I could for them.

The bell rang for seventh period to begin. I was in my office as usual straightening it up because I did not like to come back on Monday to a dirty office. I realized I heard no one running down the hall to the locker room. All of a sudden Ms. Holden, the eighth grade science teacher, knocked on my door. She was Caucasian with long red hair. She was taller than I was of course. She had big hips and thighs. She wore glasses from time to time. I later seen a tattoo on her right ankle, which led me to believe she was a live in the moment kind of person. She was cool. We became close throughout the years especially in terms of helping the students.

She had a serious look on her face. She said, "Coach something is wrong with Kiya. She is in my room very upset." Without hesitation I responded, "Take me to her." Kiya was by far the fastest athlete I have ever coach. Her speed was remarkable. She was a very quiet and shy young lady. She was what one might refer to as a "red bone." She was African-American, but had a very light skin complexion. She had gorgeous brown eyes. She never gave me any trouble on or off the court.

As I walked into Ms. Holden's room it was dark and I did not see anyone. Then all of a sudden the girls jumped up from behind the tables and yelled, "Surprise. Happy Birthday Coach. We love you." There was no use in me trying to hold back the tears because they were already rolling down my face. I was speechless. As the girls hugged me, I noticed they had a big cake with white frosting. On top it had "Happy Birthday Coach Lowery, We Love You!" It was written in cursive and in purple. They had chips, ice cream, and a bunch of presents. I looked over at Ms. Holden and before I could say anything she said, "Gotcha Coach. The girls came to me a week ago telling me what they wanted to do for you. There was no way I could resist. Happy Birthday Coach."

We took everything to the gym and continued celebrating. All of my gifts were purple. It was not anything too extravagant, but I will never forget that day. We took a ton of pictures as well. They bought a radio, hats, napkins, ice cream, and many other things. One present I will forever cherish was a white t-shirt. Willow brought it for me. Her favorite color was purple as well. She had the shirt made at the mall. The front had a Winnie the Pooh holding a bowl of honey. To the side it had black words trimmed in purple that read, "World's greatest Coach." On the back it had the same format, but read "Coach Lowery." It was officially the first surprise birthday party I ever had. I will never forget it.

The seventh grade class was taken on a field trip every year. I got asked to be a chaperone, which was fine by me because after basketball season I was bored. The girls were with the track coach preparing for track season.

His name was Coach Kane. He was a legend in Pearl. He had a street named after him and everything. He was an amazing track athlete. He was my mentor and a great one. I looked up to him and respected his opinion. He gave me good advice. Oh, he was fine too! ☺ He was tall and dark like a Hershey's kiss. He dressed nice and smelled good. He was much older than I, but he did not look it. Actually, he still ran and kept himself in shape. He was happily married as well with two outstanding children: Marcus Kane and Katrina Kane. They were exceptional athletes as well. Katrina played basketball her seventh and eighth grade year for me. We worked well together. If he seen a young lady who he thought had potential to play basketball, he told me. I did the same for him in terms of track. It also helped that he was originally from Pearl because he knew the parents and gave me the heads up on how to deal with them.

The field trip was on a Friday. I had all the basketball girls assigned to my group. I was relaxed that day. I brought my camera with me. I sat at the back of the bus to monitor the kids. The kids ended up talking to me and saying things like, "Coach everybody always saying you mean, but you the coolest teacher I know. You real and don't sugar coat anything. You got your shades on and everything. We should have got in your group."

I sat next to the window with my knees in the seat. I could not believe I was in Jackson, Mississippi on my way to the zoo *again*. Only this time I was happy. I was not alone. I had people who wanted to be around me! As all of those thoughts went through my mind, tears began to develop in my eyes. They were tears of joy this time. I kept saying, "Thank you Jesus for never forsaking me and hearing my prayers all of those years. Thank you. Thank you. I love you very much."

Once we got there and parked, one of my co-workers, who sat at the front of the bus with the rest of the teachers, stood up, faced the kids, and said, "When you get off the bus find your group teacher. You must remain with your teacher until we leave. If you want to get with another teacher you have to make sure it is okay with both teachers before doing so. If you brought your own lunch with you, leave it on the bus. We will bring you back to the bus to get it when we get ready to eat. Have fun and be careful."

My girls came running toward me as soon as they got off the bus. All of them were not in my group, but by the end of the tour they were. The zoo looked exactly the same way it did when I went in the sixth grade. Of course it was upgraded as far as some new cages and animals, but the gift store was still the same. The entrance was still the same. The only difference was that everything seemed smaller or lower to the ground, which was only because I was grown and not that little girl anymore. I had the pleasure of teaching many different children of all race. There were not many African-American teachers who worked for the district. Therefore, when Caucasian, Hispanics, and even Mexican children respected me and wanted to be around me, I was shocked. Racism was very prevalent in the district.

I had my camera and my shades and that was all I needed. It was beautiful outside. The air was crisp and refreshing. The birds were chirping. The animals in the cage were *AWAKE* and excited as we walked by. I always enjoyed seeing the pink flamingoes and peacocks. I absolutely love colors. The flamingoes were a mixture of neon pink and pastel pink. They had long pencil like legs. I took some pictures, which is another thing I love to do. The peacocks were astonishing as well, but they were allowed to roam freely. I have always been a little on edge when it came down to big birds. I always feel they will run up and attack me. Therefore, I kept my distance.

Their feathers and tails were remarkable. Dark green, blue, a touch of yellow, and a hint of black made up the feathers and tail. Some of them resembled an eye. I attempted to get a little closer and one came toward me. I immediately took off running and almost dropped my camera. The kids laughed at me so hard. I laughed as well. There was a new area that was not there before. It was a walk through cage, but it was like an aquarium. It was beautiful as well. Every location we stopped to visit I asked my group as many questions as I could to challenge and educate their minds. There were turtles, fishes, and many other aquatics. The water was as clear and blue as the water on the beach of Jamaica.

I allowed a few boys to join my group as well. They were dating some of my girls and wanted to walk with them. I thought it was the cutest thing because they were intimidated by me. Any boy who wanted to date my girls had to answer to me. I had no problem letting them know whether or not I approved of them. The girls were well aware of that. I rarely told the girls not to date a boy, but I did however, lay out the pros and cons of dating whomever they came to me about. Doing so allowed *them* to make a wise decision about selecting boyfriends.

The boys walked up to me as we were in the cage. The "chosen one," which was the one who was going to do all the talking was in the front. I continued looking at the fish and acting as if I did not see them. The chosen one, Enrique spoke, "Hey Coach Lowery." Still watching the fish and slowly walking, I said, "Hey Enrique." He continued, "Uh Coach can we join your group until we leave the zoo?"

The girls who were dating them were on the other side of me saying, "Please coach let them come with us. We will be good. Promise Coach." I continued walking and looking at the aquarium as if I was alone and did not hear them. On the other side of me were the boys, but they were walking a few feet behind me. Enrique, stepped up his pace and said, "Coach Lowery we don't get in trouble. We good boys. We not gonna be bad in your group."

I enjoyed torturing them. ☺ I looked at him and said, "Okay, you can join my group." They all got excited and began to walk toward their girlfriends. I stopped and said, "Hold up. Only one person asked me to walk with us." Before I could say anything else, the other boys came running back and individually said, "Can I walk with your group?" I said, "Yes, but keep your hands to yourself." The girls gave me a big hug and said, "Thank you Coach. You're the greatest."

We continued our journey and they behaved like they said they would. Every now and then I noticed the couples were holding hands. I cleared my throat to notify them that I seen them. They quickly let go, but only to rejoin hands from time to time throughout the visit. I thought, "That's the cutest thing. They will remember this trip for the rest of their lives. I want a smile to come across their face when they remember me." I told the kids all the time, "You may not understand why I am so tough on you now, but later on you will. And you will thank me someday."

I looked up and realized we were approaching the gift shop, which meant the tour was coming to an end. We began to see ducks and birds freely walking on the grass and pavement. The kids ran to see where they were coming from. I paused as they flew by me. My mind quickly relapsed and flashbacks appeared. It felt as if I could feel the earth rotating just as it does around the sun in the solar system. I started feeling light headed and dizzy, but managed to say, "Ya'll slow down before you fall." I knew what we were going to see next, the "tunnel." I picked one foot up at a time and placed it in front of the other. My breathing increased rapidly the closer I got. Finally, I said to myself, "What's wrong with me Jesus? That was years ago and I should be over it by now. Please do not let me faint in front of my kids. I just want to have a good time."

I made it to the tunnel, took a deep breath, and entered. All of a sudden two of my girls La'Tondra and Jenna grabbed me by the arms, one on each side and said, "Where you been coach? What took you so long? We wanna show you the snakes and spiders!" It was at that exact moment when my breathing returned to normal. The girls knew I was afraid of snakes and spiders. They were too tickled when I refused to get closer to the glass. I took pictures of them standing by the snakes. I actually enjoyed the tunnel. I saw things that were probably there when I was in the sixth grade, but I was too down to notice them. There were rats, mice, and other four-legged creatures that I did not recognize. There was a place for dead butterflies and a ton of insects! Their colors were amazing.

We made it to the actual "tunnel" where they could crawl in and put their heads in the glass window to see the ground hogs. Honestly, I am not too sure what type of animal it was, but it resembled a ground hog. La'Tondra said, "Come on coach. You know you want to get in here." I really did not. The older I got the worst my claustrophobia became. I also learned I did not like a lot of people to close to me at one time invading my space without my permission. I said, "I will be standing outside watching ya'll stick your head in. I'm gonna take pictures."

I walked outside and did just what I said. I stood there until ALL of my kids put their heads in and came out. I walked around and all the kids were on the spider web ropes. I took a lot of pictures. Janelle said, "Come in here with us coach. You short and small enough to fit. ☺" I sat down on the ropes with them, but not before giving my camera to Jenna to take a picture of me on the ropes. I felt like the kid I did not get to be the last time I was there. Everyone got up and proceeded to the gift shop. I remained in the ropes for a few extra minutes. I just laid there and savored the moment. I could not believe Jesus recreated the scene only for a different time, but better and much more deserving. I had my shades on staring at the sky.

I finally got up and walked to the gift shop. The line was long. Teachers went in with their groups. I sat outside on the long concrete bench with my girls. We talked, joked around, and took pictures until we could go inside the store. Janelle came to me and said, "Coach can we go in the store now? The line is short?" I replied, "Yeah we can go. Go tell the rest of the girls to come on."

As she went to do that, I stood and called the kids in my group who were already next to me in a huddle. Once everyone else made it and joined the huddle I said, "Ya'll are walking around representing Pearl. Act as if you have home training and were raised right when we go in this store. Do not play around. Do not touch it if you are not gonna buy it. Do not break line when paying for your item. If you do not want to go in the store or go in and don't see anything you like, come back outside and sit in our area until we all come out. Do not run all around the zoo or you might get left. Do ya'll understand me?" As a group they collectively said, "Yes ma'am." Playfully and with a big smile, I said, "Let's go then."

The store was very small. Seeing as to how my favorite color is purple, everything that had purple in it caught my attention. The kids were excited. From time to time I walked over to the window to check on the ones who did not come in. They were doing exactly what I told them to. I started back walking around. The kids were coming to me trying to show me what they brought. I ended up not buying anything, but as we walked out I thought to myself, "Now that Jesus has blessed me with the money to get whatever I wanted out of that store, I don't even want anything. Ain't that something!"

We sat down until all the other groups went in the store. Then something remarkable happened. The girls began to walk up to me one at a time with gifts for *me*! La'Tondra said, "Coach it ain't much, but its purple. I hope you like it." It was a purple pen. The tears began to fill my eyes. No one had ever brought something for me without me telling them to. For those girls to remember me saying purple was my favorite color was unbelievable. It told me one thing, "They really did *LISTEN* to me when I had those talks with them."

Little things mean more to me than big things. "It's the little things that count." I ended up with key chains, cup holders, and all kind of things. I still have them because I do not believe in getting rid of things that mean a lot to me. On our way back to the school I looked out the window and said, "Faith is believing in the unseen. All you need is faith the size of a mustard seed. Jesus I don't know how I kept the faith, but I did after all these years. Thank you from the bottom of my heart."

CHAPTER 32

Personal Perceptions

Seeing as to how spiritual I am, that is *spiritual* not *religious*, there is a difference. There are many questions and thoughts that cross my mind from time to time. I question atheists, homosexuality, adultery, bullying, suicide, and many other topics. The number one question that has pondered my mind for years is how is it that *EVERYTHING* Jesus wrote in the bible for us not to do, we do? Look at the Ten Commandments. Everyone has disobeyed most if not all of them. Train a child in the way he/she should go; spare the rod spoil the child, yet in today's society a parent can be thrown into jail for whipping their child and schools no longer have corporal punishment. Prayer is not allowed in schools anymore and we wonder why when children reach adulthood they have no strong morals, ethics, or values. Not every child has a family who attends church or practice spirituality or religion for that matter.

In terms of homosexuality, a young lady Aiesha, who was gay in the eighth grade said, "Coach Lowery my momma criticize me and say I'm going to hell cause I'm gay. I go to church and love going, but comments like that make me not want to go. The bible says God loves all of us and John 3:16 basically says whoever believes that Jesus was God's son and believes in Him will have eternal life. I seen the scripture about homosexuality. At first it bothered me, but now it doesn't. It's no different than any other scripture. I am who I am and it was hard for me to come to terms with that, but once I accepted it I realized how happy I was. I finally asked my momma did she really think I would choose to be gay and receive the torture and humiliation from people. If in fact gay people go to hell, why would I choose to be gay? Gay chose me!"

I thought about what she said. She had a point and I use to wonder the same thing. I have always been the kind of person who kept an open mind. I did not care what a person did or who they were as long as they did not cause harm or bother me.

I have always wanted to meet an atheist. I mean a real one to see how they live on a day to day basis without believing in something or being spiritual. I always try to educate myself on as much as possible regardless of what it is. Out of all the things I have been through and the times when I got mad at Jesus and *TRIED* to get Him out of my life, I still talked and prayed to Him daily. It kept me sane, focused, and positive.

Do atheists go to heaven? Does a woman who cheats on her husband go to heaven? When a person commits suicide, do they go to heaven? The bible says if a person repents, confess their sins, and ask for forgiveness, they will be saved and can enter the gates of heaven. Does a couple who lives together before getting married go to heaven? Children dishonor and disobey their parents constantly. Do they go to hell? The King James Bible says there is only one God, the alpha and omega. Today there are many different types of religions. Will the people of all those religions go to hell?

I know I may be raising all kind of eyebrows in terms of my personality and spirituality, but one thing that I have learned especially from the bullying I have dealt with, is to speak my mind. Do not be afraid of what people will think of me or say about me. If I strike a nerve it is because I am telling the truth or asking what everyone else wants to ask, but are afraid to. It is not *what* you say, but *how* you say it. I am not criticizing, judging, or questioning the bible. I am merely allowing what is in my mind to be seen by the world as well as saying what others are afraid to say.

I read the bible every day that I can and I actually understand it, but when I walk through the gates of heaven and see Jesus we are going to have a long talk. The people behind me are going to just have to get mad because I am going to "have a little talk with Jesus and tell him all about my troubles." I see us sitting outside in a field of beautiful green grass drinking strawberry or blueberry Kool-Aid talking about the things that I had to endure on earth. I probably already know what His responses will be, but it will give me closure to actually be in His presence and see Him face to face.

Another question that burns me up inside is all the controversy over whether or not Jesus was black or white. What difference does it make as long as He answers prayers and continue to prove himself time and time again! I mean really what difference does it make? If He brings a person out of financial burden, health problems, mental illness, marriage and family problems, among many other issues and challenges that life throws at us, who cares what His skin color or hair texture was! God loves everybody and I truly believe that anyone regardless of who they are or what they have done, if they repent and believe in Jesus, they will go to heaven. The only people who I cannot too much see going to heaven are those who sexually abuse children and murderers, but then again God loves everybody and forgives everybody.

My second year teaching I pulled into the parking lot of my residence, which was an apartment complex. I was tired and exhausted because I had just coached a basketball game. As I was about to get out of my car, my cell phone rang. It was Biancca, my little sister. No matter how tired or busy I was, I always made time for her. What I heard on the other end of that call tore me to pieces.

I answered, "Hello." The voice was momma's instead. Her voice had concern and worry in it. She said, "Ketta talk to Biancca and calm her down. Talk to her and tell her how you were picked on and bullied when you were in school. The kids been picking on her." I heard Biancca in the background crying and very upset.

A million things ran through my mind at that moment. The most obvious one was, "You knew the entire time what those kids were doing to me, your child and you said nor done nothing! All these years I thought no one paid enough attention to me to even realize what I was going through." Then I thought, "Where were you? Why did you not do anything?"

By then Biancca was on the phone. I felt helpless and the fact that I could not hug her nor pray with her at that exact moment ate away at my soul. The tears began to roll down my face. She was crying as though someone had died. I took a deep breath and said, "Calm down and tell me what's going on. Who picking on you? What kind of things they say about you?"

I heard her wiping the tears, blowing her nose, and clearing her throat. Finally she responded, "Jacey be talking bout me to everybody. The girls on the basketball team don't like me. Boys say I'm ugly." All of a sudden my compassion turned to rage. My little sister was getting "bullied" and I did not know. The fact that I lived an hour away from her made me my rage increase even more. How could I not know? She and I talk about EVERYTHING. In the back of my mind as she got older, I always knew she would probably deal with getting teased because of her weight, but her personality always out shined any flaws she may have had. I knew as she got older the weight would disappear anyway. She never seemed to care what others thought of her. I always envied that.

She is tall and takes well after her father's side of the family when it comes down to physical appearance. The older she gets the more she grows into her frame just as I suspected of course. Her hips and thighs mesh well into her upper torso. Her skin complexion is dark brown. She is a Libra meaning she has a high sense for fashion. She loves to shop and accessorize. She loves getting her nails and hair done. When her and Ardeshia get together, they are unstoppable is terms of fashion.

Even though I was pissed off and ready to go to Ethel High School and beat the hell out of those evil kids, I quickly calmed myself down and snapped back to reality. She was thirteen at the time. It was her first year at the high school. I said, "Kids your age do and say stupid stuff that they will one day live to regret. Don't worry about Jacey. She just wants to fit in and doing whatever she can to be a part of a click. Boys will be boys and

I promise you the girl they say is a 10 will be a 2 ten years from now. You are smart and beautiful inside and out. You got a heart of gold just like me. Keep praying and believing because things will get better. What's going on with Jacey anyway?"

Jacey had been her best-friend since pre-kindergarten. I have a ton of pictures with those two side by side. She was a tall skinny light skin African-American girl. She had shoulder length hair brown. She was the baby of her family as well with the exception of a little brother. She had other siblings my age just like Biancca. They were inseparable.

Biancca said, "Ketta I don't know what's wrong with her. She disobedient towards her parents. She gets mad and slam doors in their face. She talking to older boys. They don't care about her. I told her that, but she won't listen. The girls she hang around talk about her behind her back. They say she nasty. They just use her and she can't even see it. She not the same. I don't even like being around her anymore."

Before I responded I thought, "Jesus thank you for allowing me to raise a magnificent young lady. She is a leader who is not afraid to follow her own path in life." I said, "I love you and I am very proud of you. Keep making good grades and everything will pay off. I always pray for you. I will always be here no matter what. As long as nobody put their hands on you do your best to overlook it. But if somebody tries to fight, you defend yourself. Jesus keep certain people away from you for a reason, remember that. I love you." By then she had calmed all the way down. We were cracking jokes and laughing. I felt relieved to see her personality come back into play. She said, "I love you too. Talk to you later."

Before I got out of my car I sat there to let everything absorb in. I cried and prayed:

> "Jesus I have done all I can when it comes down to my baby. I love her more than anything. I know I raised her right. Most importantly I raised her to know *YOU*. For that I am forever grateful. Please keep your angels around her as protection. Give her the inspiration to pursue her hopes and dreams. Let nothing stand in her way. Bless me to be there for her in every way possible no matter what. Grant me the serenity to accept the things I cannot change (others), the courage to change what I can (me), and the wisdom to know the difference. I love you Jesus, Amen."

coachlowery@ymail.com or the bullying challenge on Facebook

CPSIA information can be obtained at www.ICGtesting.com
Printed in the USA
LVOW081713240412

278949LV00008B/19/P